Joint-Use Libraries

Joint-Use Libraries has been co-published simultaneously as *Resource Sharing & Information Networks*, Volume 15, Numbers 1/2 2001.

T0314690

Joint-Use Libraries

William Miller
Rita M. Pellen
Editors

Joint-Use Libraries has been co-published simultaneously as *Resource Sharing & Information Networks*, Volume 15, Numbers 1/2 2001.

Routledge
Taylor & Francis Group
New York   London

First published by:

The Haworth Information Press®,10 Alice Street,Binghamton, NY 13904-1580 USA

The Haworth Information Press® is an imprint of The Haworth Press, Inc., 10 Alice Street, Binghamton, NY 13904-1580 USA.

This edition published 2012 by Routledge:

Routledge	Routledge
Taylor & Francis Group	Taylor & Francis Group
711 Third Avenue	2 Park Square, Milton Park
New York, NY 10017	Abingdon, Oxon OX14 4RN

Joint-Use Libraries **has been co-published simultaneously as Resource Sharing & Information Networks, Volume 15, Numbers 1/2 2001.**

The development, preparation, and publication of this work has been undertaken with great care. However, the publisher, employees, editors, and agents of The Haworth Press and all imprints of The Haworth Press, Inc., including The Haworth Medical Press® and Pharmaceutical Products Press®,are not responsible for any errors contained herein or for consequences that may ensue from use of materials or information contained in this work. Opinions expressed by the author(s) are not necessarily those of The Haworth Press, Inc. With regard to case studies, identities and circumstances of individuals discussed herein have been changed to protect confidentiality. Any resemblance to actual persons, living or dead, is entirely coincidental.

Cover design by Brooke R. Stiles.

Library of Congress Cataloging-in-Publication Data

Joint-use libraries / William Miller, Rita M. Pellen, editors,
        p. cm.
Co-published simultaneously as Resource sharing & information networks, v. 15, no. 1/2,2001.
        Includes bibliographical references and index.
        ISBN 0-7890-2070-X (alk. paper) - ISBN 0-7890-2071-8 (pbk.: alk. paper)
        1. Joint-use libraries-Case studies. I. Miller, William, 1947-. II. Pellen, Rita M. III. Resource sharing & information networks.
Z675.J64J65 2003
021.6'4-dc21
                                                    2003000040

Joint-Use Libraries

CONTENTS

ABOUT THE EDITORS

William Miller, PhD, MLS, is Director of Libraries at Florida Atlantic University. He formerly served as Head of Reference at Michigan State University and as Associate Dean of Libraries at Bowling Green State University in Ohio. Dr. Miller is Past-President of the Association of College and Research Libraries, has served as Chair of the *Choice* Editorial Board, and is a frequent contributor to professional journals in addition to being a contributing editor of *Library Issues*. Dr. Miller also teaches courses in English literature.

Rita M. Pellen, MLS, is Associate Director of Libraries at Florida Atlantic University, where she previously served as Assistant Director of Public Services and Head of the Reference Department. In 1993, she received the Gabor Exemplary Employee Award in recognition for outstanding service to the university, and in 1997 she received the "Literati Club Award for Excellence" for her outstanding paper published in *The Bottom Line*. She has served on committees in LAMA, ACRL, and ALCTS, as well as the Southeast Florida Library Information Network (SEFLIN), a multi-type library cooperative in south Florida. Her honor society memberships include Beta Phi Mu and Phi Kappa Pi.

Introduction

The old cliche about cooperation being "an unnatural act" does not apply to librarians, to judge from the articles in this collection. Indeed, just the opposite seems to be the case; librarians, regardless of where they are, always seem to generate a wide variety of cooperative activities, locally, regionally, nationally, and even internationally, in the process creating a bewildering array of organizations and acronyms. Over and over again, the readers of this volume will see librarians coming together in ways that would simply not occur in other fields. The truth of that observation was brought home to me several years ago during one of our quarterly meetings of the state university system library directors in Florida. At this particular meeting, we decided to invite a faculty member from each institution to discuss collection development issues with us. One of those faculty members, the chair of a history department, said "You librarians are light years ahead of us. It would never even occur to the state university system history department chairs to meet about common issues."

Cooperation used to mean primarily cataloging via OCLC, interlibrary loan, and perhaps mutual borrowing privileges, but economics and technology are combining to broaden the playing field considerably. In this volume, we highlight one growing aspect of cooperation: the joint-use library, which in some ways is the ultimate expression of cooperation, in that libraries of different types literally amalgamate to serve two or more different populations in the same facility, with a combined staff, in ways which are transparent to the user.

Economics is probably the primary factor behind the growing trend, in which two or more entities come together to form a library that offers collections and services that neither could have afforded to offer indi-

[Haworth co-indexing entry note]: "Introduction." Miller, William. Co-published simultaneously in *Resource Sharing & Information Networks* (The Haworth Information Press, an imprint of The Haworth Press, Inc.) Vol. 15, No. 1/2, 2001, pp. 1-4; and: *Joint-Use Libraries* (ed: William Miller, and Rita M. Pellen) The Haworth Information Press, an imprint of The Haworth Press, Inc., 2001, pp. 1-4. Single or multiple copies of this article are available for a fee from The Haworth Document Delivery Service [1-800-HAWORTH, 9:00 a.m. - 5:00 p.m. (EST). E-mail address: getinfo@haworthpress.com].

10.1300/J121v15n01_01

vidually. Building a library today is typically a multi-million dollar venture which may be an unaffordable proposition for a smaller city or academic institution. Under such circumstances, organizations are more and more willing to come together to build one physical library that serves multiple constituencies, recognizing in advance that differing missions and cultures will lead to conflict and differences that will have to be overcome, but accepting these problems in advance as an acceptable price to pay for the synergistic benefits that occur when resources are pooled.

This model of sharing library facilities between different institutions was common years ago in rural areas of Michigan and elsewhere, where school libraries doubled also as public library facilities. Sharon Honig-Bear illustrates that this kind of partnership is still very much alive in her article about Washoe County, Nevada, where the County School District, along with the Nevada Division of Wildlife, have joined in a three-way partnership with the county to provide library services to the population of this rural area, thereby making maximum use of the resources of all partners to provide something beyond the ability of any single one to offer.

Kathleen Imhoff provides an overview and details of the permutations of Broward County Public Library's partnerships with university, community college, public and private school libraries within South Florida. Even though these cooperative ventures present challenges concerning governance, financing, staffing, security, and technology integration issues, there is substantial evidence that joint-use facilities are advantageous to the partnering libraries and the communities they serve.

The fastest-growing trend now is for academic libraries (community college and university) or academic and public libraries to come together in a variety of ways. Several articles in this volume illustrate models of community college/university cooperation. Julia Woods writes about a joint library in Davie, Florida, located on the campus of Broward Community College, funded equally by BCC and Florida Atlantic University, and serving the students and faculty of both institutions because FAU has a campus within BCC's campus. In this library, all employees, including the director, work officially for BCC, but work collegially with the faculty and administrators of both institutions. In a similar arrangement, Cynthia Fugate describes the joint library serving the University of Washington campus at Bothell and Cascadia Community College. Both institutions are located on the same physical campus, and had been instructed from their inception to share facilities whenever possible. In this case, the university is the primary provider of library services under contract with the community college.

More complex arrangements are also becoming common. Patricia Roshaven and Rudy Widman write about a three-way library in Pt. St. Lucie, Florida, in which a community college, a university, and a public library each contributes its own staffing, collections, and other resources to offer services in a small but growing community where none of the entities alone could have afforded to build a first-rate facility. In this shared facility, there is as yet no director, and a team-based strategy is employed to make most decisions. James Olliver and Susan Anderson write about another complex situation in which St. Petersburg College and the City of Seminole, Florida are building a joint-use facility which will serve not only the city and the college on a newly-created campus, but will also serve the students of 14 other institutions of higher education which will be invited to offer courses at this new campus in order to give local residents a wide variety of educational options without leaving home.

This volume features 9 different models of joint-use library arrangements; the wide variety of organizational schemes shows that there is no one way to run a joint-use library. Which library's online catalog will be used? How will costs for maintenance and utilities be shared? Will there be one integrated staff, or two separate staffs inhabiting the same building? There is no simple answer to these questions, and the answers differ from project to project. The libraries described range from the very small library described by Karen A. Dornseif that is shared by Front Range Community College and the City of Fort Collins, Colorado, to the mammoth new joint library now being built in San Jose, California. Christina Peterson and Patricia Senn Breivik describe this $177.5 million project, in which the City of San Jose and San Jose State University are building what amounts to a new main library for both institutions, one in which some services will be integrated, while others will be retained by one or the other of the staffs of the two institutions.

In other models, such as that at Nova University and the Broward County Library described by Harriett MacDougall and Nora Quinlan, one institution is clearly the senior partner, but a largely new, integrated staff has been hired to minimize resistance to the new joint mission, and to serve all users equally. As Dornseif says, "There is no model joint-use library. Each reflects not only the institutional culture, mission, and circumstances of every partner, but the unique combination of these in a shared facility." Readers may examine the variety of models presented here and decide for themselves which is likely to work best in any given situation.

William Miller
Director of Libraries
Florida Atlantic University

School-Public Library Partnerships in Washoe County, Nevada

Sharon Honig-Bear

SUMMARY. Washoe County Library and the Washoe County School District developed partnership libraries (public libraries using public schools during non-school hours) as a creative approach to library service and resource sharing in tight economic times. With sites at two elementary schools, three middle schools and two high schools, Washoe County discovered that students, teachers, and the public gain enhanced services and resources. The article focuses on site and staff selection, building standards, contract responsibilities, and funding. *[Article copies available for a fee from The Haworth Document Delivery Service: 1-800-HAWORTH. E-mail address: <getinfo@haworthpress.com> Website: <http://www.HaworthPress.com> © 2001 by The Haworth Press, Inc. All rights reserved.]*

KEYWORDS. Joint-use libraries, library cooperation, community libraries, school-public library cooperation, partnership libraries, innovative approaches to library service

Sharon Honig-Bear, MLS, has been Development Officer at Washoe County Library system for 12 years. She is primarily responsible for grant writing and other fundraising activities in this rapidly growing library system. She has been an active participant in the growth and funding of partnership libraries.

Address correspondence to: Sharon Honig-Bear, P.O. Box 2151, Reno, NV 89505 (E-mail: shonig@mail.co.washoe.nv.us).

[Haworth co-indexing entry note]: "School-Public Library Partnerships in Washoe County, Nevada." Honig-Bear, Sharon. Co-published simultaneously in *Resource Sharing & Information Networks* (The Haworth Information Press, an imprint of The Haworth Press, Inc.) Vol. 15, No. 1/2, 2001, pp. 5-16; and: *Joint-Use Libraries* (ed: William Miller, and Rita M. Pellen) The Haworth Information Press, an imprint of The Haworth Press, Inc., 2001, pp. 5-16. Single or multiple copies of this article are available for a fee from The Haworth Document Delivery Service [1-800-HAWORTH, 9:00 a.m. - 5:00 p.m. (EST). E-mail address: getinfo@haworthpress.com].

10.1300/J121v15n01_02

Experience is a hard teacher because she gives the test first, the lesson afterwards.

–variously attributed

The staff of Washoe County Library (Reno, Nevada) have considerable experience in school-public partnership libraries. Hundreds of libraries from New Zealand to Germany to Australia and Alaska have contacted us about partnership libraries, especially school-public joint-use facilities. We hear from architects, planners, developers, and school districts. We've spoken at conferences, provided site tours to visitors from other communities and created a website http://www.washoe.lib.nv.us/yypartr.html.

We've been busy, since 1986, expanding service to six isolated communities (including one in our inner city) without a nearby public library, by using a partnership model. We don't spend a lot of time conducting research or analyzing the effectiveness of partnership libraries (although we encourage others to study this). As described by Washoe County Library Director Nancy Cummings, "We've had to work hard building and maintaining good relations with our partners. We've had some challenges and overcome most of them. We'd like to think that our experience can help others understand a public library viewpoint. If we're experts, it's because we've lived to tell the tale!"

MEETING COMMUNITY NEEDS
AND YIELDING BIG BENEFITS

Many who are seriously considering developing a partnership for a new library are probably faced with providing more services in your community while facing budget reductions.

This has been the situation in Washoe County for a long time and we've found that partnership libraries are a useful tool to reach more people in tough budget times. We got into the "partnership library business" primarily as a way to connect with outlying communities (which we typically define as a location more than 5 miles from an existing library) with no extra money in sight (especially for facilities). Despite the compromises and challenges, operating a partnership library offers a formula as an economically feasible way to provide library service where none exists.

Who exactly have been our partners? Washoe County School District (WCSD, the second largest district in Nevada, enrolling over 57,000 students) has been our primary partner, with library sites at two elementary schools, three middle schools, and two high schools at different times.

Developing a partnership with the public schools was natural since the schools are conveniently located throughout the County and because we share somewhat similar missions to educate the community.

Recently, the Nevada Division of Wildlife joined us in a three-way partnership to create a community library/nature center in a scenic but isolated town at the Nevada-California border. We also have a cooperative arrangement that provides a small but full-service library in the Washoe County Senior Center. Washoe County Library has a number of other collaborative projects, including one with the local arts organization which manages several art galleries in Library facilities.

Washoe County, Nevada is home to 339,486 people, most of whom live in the metropolitan Reno-Sparks area. Like Nevada overall, we've been experiencing major growth (the population saw approximately a 30% increase from 1990 to 2000) and new housing developments appear at the blink of an eye. This new development, unfortunately, doesn't pay for itself in terms of concurrency, and community services such as libraries and schools scramble to fund the services generated by growth. To meet these growing needs, we successfully passed a 30-year tax initiative in 1994 and a library bond in 2000. Our Mobile Library service, begun in 2001, brings resources to urban areas, primarily to pre-schools and low-income neighborhoods where people may find it difficult to get to a library. To this mix, we add partnership libraries as a good response, a creative approach to library service in tight economic times.

The benefits of partnership libraries are numerous and exciting. In a variety of ways–from computers, to increased collections to increased hours of access–students, teachers and the public gain enhanced services and resources. As Ellen Fockler, WCSD's Library Coordinator says, "When the books come to the kids in the partnership libraries, we break down barriers for them to get what they need." Another good reason, of course, for partnership libraries is that agency boards and administrators look good when they cooperate and maximize resources. Joint-use libraries put into action the goal of many governments to bring about change collaboratively. And the public notices. An editorial published in the *Reno Gazette Journal* said, after groundbreaking for our three-way partnership in Verdi, "The collaboration between the Washoe County School District, Washoe County Library System, the Nevada Wildlife Division and the community is a model of how pooling resources can result in a project bigger and better than what each agency could do alone."

Some years ago, we jotted down *Ten Good Things about School/Public Partnership Libraries:*

1. they're cost effective because they share facilities and resources
2. they bring public libraries to new areas without funding for new buildings
3. staff gets a great opportunity for professional growth and diverse duties
4. they're a model of collaboration
5. they relieve crowding at other libraries
6. they give the public more library choices and locations
7. school library staff see a wider range in ages of library users
8. they encourage reading and literacy
9. students and teachers have more options for library materials
10. the technology in joint-use libraries is better than school libraries can afford

As good a list as this is, recently a school staffer mentioned a new benefit. She believes that children are increasing their knowledge of the public library system through the joint-use facilities. Instead of the limitations found in most school libraries, children are exposed to the extensive collections and the sophisticated technology of the public library. These youngsters are leaving public school with a working knowledge about how public libraries operate. And all the children are already equipped with their own library card!

By the way, we've called these special libraries different names over time. We tried using the term "joint-use" library–but found it awkward, not "poetic" enough. For a while we called our collaborative libraries "partnership" libraries. Eventually we coined the phrase "community library" to distinguish the facilities that are operated jointly with another institution. We hope that the name puts out a welcome mat to the neighborhood and communicates that the Library is not just for children.

Economic factors aren't the most important measure of success for joint-use libraries, as we've come to learn. We're excited about how joint-use libraries allow us to touch people's lives. These libraries improve the quality of life for residents who live near them. Our positive reaction to joint-use libraries is based on one simple thing: the community is responding to us.

Just to give you some idea of their use, in the past year alone, the sites have increased their "index of activity" (our statistical measure that counts people in the library, circulation figures and reference questions) by 32%. If we take the comparison back to FY 1998-99 and compare it to 2001-2002 statistics, we are pleased to see a 77% increase in use of our partnership sites.

IS A PARTNERSHIP LIBRARY RIGHT
FOR YOUR COMMUNITY?

Are you ready to begin a formal partnership? Are you ready to embark on a long-term relationship which requires communication and cooperation, the keys to success? Some of the key points in establishing and operating a partnership library:

1. Investigate if the timing and climate are right for a partnership. Community support is essential and grass roots efforts can spark the project. Conducting a survey in the community is a good idea.
2. Your chances for success increase when all partners "buy in" to the idea. Administrators and Board must be enthusiastic to give you the foundation to meet any challenges that arise.
3. The partnership concept works equally well in rural, suburban or inner-city neighborhoods.
4. Planning and coordination take time and effort. Have a long-range plan that is mutually beneficial to all partners.
5. Develop a contract (memo of understanding or some written document) that outlines the role each partner will play. Partners help develop and examine contracts, policies and procedures.
6. The public library typically opens after school, evenings and on weekends. Many problems will be eliminated by having mutually exclusive hours for the public and school patrons.
7. Library collections reflect the demographics and interest of the community. The school and the public librarian each administers its own budget and selects materials. Generally we work to develop different parts of the collections. For example, in our elementary school sites, the school uses its budget to purchase library materials appropriate for its students. The public library supplements the school collection by purchasing materials for pre-schoolers, young adults and adults. These are general guidelines, although the public library typically has more budget and will often cover special needs to serve its community.

FOUR QUICK LESSONS FOR SUCCESS

As the quote used at the top of this article indicates, we've passed the test but have been busy learning the lessons for the past ten years. Here are four big lessons we've learned:

Lesson one: Select your site carefully and make sure it's large enough for the community and to accommodate growth.

When we first plunged into the partnership library business, we were happy to be providing ANY public service. As a result, we overlooked the space and physical limitations of the facilities. While an optimistic viewpoint is essential to make joint-use facilities work, overlooking obvious red flags (like inadequate space and sometimes resistant staff) creates problems down the line.

At our Verdi Community Library, for example, we opened in a 900 sq. ft. classroom which had to function as both the school and public library. No wonder, after only a short time, a grass roots effort arose in the community to enlarge the facility. The room was so small that computers remained in boxes. There was no room for comfortable, adult-sized seating. Although any item in the public library catalog could be brought to Verdi within days of a hold being placed, the permanent collection was severely limited. Unfortunately, there was no other space in the school to move the Library. Over time, the community helped us fund raise, we acquired a second partner with the Nevada Division of Wildlife, and we patched together the $700,000 needed to fund a new, free-standing Community Library and Nature Center that will open late 2002. The facility still has less space than hoped (it's under 4,000 sq. ft.) but will be a great improvement with its meeting room space, expanded shelving, room for multiple purposes, a workroom, better amenities for staff, etc.

Compare this "making do" scenario with our later experiences in which we created a partnership library ONLY when the facility was large enough. At the Mendive Community Library, for example, we worked with the school district from the beginning as they planned a new middle school with a library that would be large enough to meet school and public needs. We incorporated important features such as a visible entrance directly into the Library from the outside (instead of directing the public through the school), adequate and convenient parking, good outside lighting (since expanded public hours mean the libraries are now used in the evening), and signage to inform the neighborhood that the public library is open for business. We recommend these basics to anyone considering a partnership library.

This planning has paid off and Mendive Community Library is one of our showcase sites. We have the space to offer a specialized children's area and this has prompted a variety of special programming. The collection is large and has drawn a devoted following of local adults. The partnership has been so successful that the library will remain even though funding to build a new public library in the general region came through a library bond issue passed in 2000. The Library is circulating over 88,000 items a year, with over 60,000 visits to the Library. It's clear that this local partnership library has pleased its public— and is here to stay.

Lesson two: It's important to assemble the right staff team. It's best to open joint-use libraries in environments with flexible staff who see the benefits of sharing resources.

If there's one vital point we've learned, it's that partnership libraries work best when you've assembled the right staff team. As Ellen Fockler mentions, "Staff relations are probably the most fragile issue. The libraries are working from different perspectives and their points of view need to be respected." Excellent communication skills are essential because staff need to express priorities and needs and even peeves.

The best approach is to hire the right people. One public librarian pointed out that administrators should hire people who like teamwork, with "emotional maturity." In our district, school principals select their school librarian; however, we find that most principals will accept input from public library staff in selecting a compatible match. In our best cases, partners are actually present during the interviewing and hiring. We've also discovered that staff need to be supervised, evaluated, and paid directly by their partnership agency (at one time our public library staff received their checks through the school district).

Planning the physical space for staff can also reduce problems. In several of our sites, the office space was so limited that staff were compromised in their comfort. Some even needed to share desks. These circumstances make it difficult to be good neighbors on a long-term basis.

Careful use of the calendar will also offset conflict. Communication about school holidays, summer vacations, etc., is essential to ensure smooth operation of the public library. In our early partnership years, small but annoying problems arose during school vacations. When public library staff arrived to open the Library, they might find that the building's heat was turned way down or that maintenance was scheduled in the building. These types of problems fell away as communication improved.

A special warning if you're considering converting an existing school site: assess carefully the interest of the principal and the school librarian in creating the partnership. It's not easy to gauge the inner feelings of staff but a careful analysis of their flexibility, ability to embrace change, and carry a positive, solution-oriented approach to library management will go a long way in avoiding trouble in the future.

We've had some experience with pre-existing staff resenting change in "their" library. These types of territorial issues are difficult to resolve and over time, may only be satisfied with a change of personnel. Because library administrators and school principals need to work together to establish trust and support staff, it's important that they too show strong commitment to making partnerships work. They will be the troubleshooters when problems arise.

Lesson three: Establish standards for a comfortable, self-contained library and have a contract that outlines responsibilities.

Over time, we decided to enter partnerships only if they had a reasonable chance of meeting community needs. As a result, we established standards that outline the essential elements that must be present in the school (or other) facility to make it an acceptable site. Beyond physical requirements for the site, the standards include provisions for hiring, allocating time for non-desk time, communication, and staff training.

In addition, we have a contract that outlines the partners' financial and other obligations. In our case, the public library is committed to providing staff for the public hours, computer equipment, access to the library's catalog (currently through Dynix) and other necessary equipment, if not available through the school. We outfit the Library with an opening day collection and, importantly, a budget for continuing collection development. We provide delivery service to each facility several times weekly, bringing them items they have placed on hold from other library locations. We provide professional support (Washoe County Library oversees cataloging and processing for both school and public collections, for example) and training for both partner staff. Although it varies from library to library, we also offer programming for the whole family.

The schools' largest contribution, of course, is the physical site, which means they also pay for the utilities and cleaning services. They are also responsible for maintaining the facility and providing adequate shelving and security. Other needs include a compatible book detection system, proper lighting, access for people with disabilities, and designated bathrooms. The schools provide materials suitable for the curriculum and staff to provide service during school hours.

Despite a contract, flexibility still remains critical. If, for example, a library has a need for shelving and there is no money in the school budget to provide it, we haven't stood firm. The public library has stepped in numerous times to assist. Through grants, private gifts and a steady stream of support from the Friends of Washoe County Library, we have improved service regardless of the strict confines of the contract. Some responsibilities (both interior and exterior signage, for example) may be shared by both partners.

Lesson four: Funding for start-up costs is relatively easy to find. The real challenge is to ensure on-going operating funds and to make sure the budget has the capacity to grow.

The collaborative nature of these libraries brings start-up costs within reach. Funders consider them "sexy." It helps that you can demonstrate that a whole new community that was previously underserved by libraries will get access. We've had success with LSTA funding, private foundations, and community appeals.

We underestimated the costs, however, to keep the libraries open. When we first began—and with no standards for service—we cut corners. We "underfilled" the public library positions, filling them with talented, but low-ranking, library assistants. Eventually we realized that these staff had responsibilities equal to any small library manager and we needed to address pay equity issues. We also had to acknowledge other issues such as staff safety (partnership libraries now have a minimum of two staff present when they're open to the public, a standard used in our other libraries), adding to the expense of operating partnership libraries. There is good value with partnership libraries but they aren't as inexpensive as we first thought.

COORDINATION AND COMMUNICATION

Big issues such as security and filtering do come up and a track record for good communication between partners will help tremendously. It's a good idea to distinguish between issues that are common to all the partnership libraries and which issues are site-specific. Either way, it's good to create a way for the decision-makers representing each partner to meet on a regular basis to build rapport and to troubleshoot.

Coordination among the partners is the key. While we have periodic meetings of school and public library staff, our simplest situation has been for the senior administrator from each partner to meet to coordinate service; each will then communicate to his or her staff. This simple solution replaces more complex mechanisms (we had a Partnership Advisory Committee for several years that included representatives from the community as well as the partners–but they lacked the authority to make policy or bring about change). As Ellen Fockler says, "The greatest difficulty comes when we're not willing to listen to each other."

One large issue is student safety. This issue is especially important from the school's point of view, as it struggles with "lockdowns" and family crises. At one of our partnership libraries in an elementary school site, staff expressed their concern that having unknown adults in the Library during the day raises security questions and a concern for the well-being of the students. As a result, typically our partnership sites are closed to the public during the school day, even though this limits the effectiveness of the partnership library for the adult user. This is one of the important compromises we've made to honor the partnership relationship. Happily, safety is less of an issue as children get older and we have more flexibility in our middle and high school locations.

Another on-going issue is access to information. While no one is advocating censorship, public schools and public libraries often differ in how they build their collections. School-public partnerships may be the most difficult ones to maneuver through this issue; public libraries partnering with community colleges and other adult-based sites may avoid these types of conflicts.

While both schools and public libraries want to serve their users, finding a comfortable middle ground for service can take some compromise. In our elementary school sites, we've found that separating the adult and children's collections helps. That way, during school hours, the librarian can direct children to appropriate materials in the juvenile section. The room's layout helps focus kids' attention on appropriate materials. School librarians have expressed that they would like to see more restraint in book selection from public librarians. This attitude can be embraced by the public librarian too. As one said, "We have a responsibility to be sensitive to our partners." Another important compromise accepted by the public library is that all Internet stations in the partnership libraries are filtered.

Like any on-going relationship, partners need to work at it. We try to keep our eye on the big picture and remind ourselves that the small compromises we make allow us to enhance neighborhoods continually. We try to remember that the alternative to these partnership facilities may be *no library service at all*. With service to the public in mind, it's always been very clear which option we prefer.

SUCCESS CREATES OPPORTUNITIES

The Duncan/Traner Community Library is one of our more success-ful sites. Located in an inner-city area isolated by highways, the low-in-come families in this area have found it difficult to get to other library locations. In 1994 we opened a partnership library in Traner Middle School. We knew the facility was inadequate but we were pleased to es-tablish library services in that community, while continuing to search for funding to build a free-standing facility. Working with the School District, we wrote a federal block grant which gave us funding in 1997 for a 4,000 sq. ft. modular structure, located between Duncan Elemen-tary and Traner Middle schools.

The building is visible to everyone in the community and has been a successful gathering spot for children and families in the neighborhood. Community response to the Library continues to be excellent. In FY 2000-01, for example, we saw a 16% increase in activity at the Duncan/Traner Community Library. Programming at the Library has increased by 40%, offering everything from bi-lingual storytimes to a Library sleepover that attracted 29 children ages 7-14. Last year, we were even able to use the talents of an Americorps volunteer to do art-work with the children and create a colorful mural in the facility. Children and young adults love the Library for its computers and tech-nology; in this low-income neighborhood, the library offers an easy link to technology for many of the youth.

BE PREPARED TO RESPOND TO CHANGE

We've had several changes in our partnership libraries over the years. Part of our success comes from the partners involving communi-ties and then continuing to revise the plan for the best ways to serve them–even if that means significant change. We've found listening to the public (all of our libraries distribute a simple survey that provides regular feedback about what library users like and need) has taken us in new directions.

Two of our sites were created with the hope that they were a "tempo-rary fix" until we could build a full-service, independent branch of the Washoe County Library system. When we first opened the partnership facilities, we had no guarantee that we'd find the money to build alter-natives. Eventually we were able to fund both of the new facilities through hard-earned, voter-approved initiatives. One of these partner-ships closed in 1999 with the opening of a 30,000 sq. ft. Northwest

Reno Library and another will close in 2003 when we open the 18,000 sq. ft. South Valleys Library.

Two of our sites described here, in Verdi and Duncan/Traner, started in small spaces within public schools but have since moved to larger, free-standing buildings on school property. Again, creative financing (grants and community appeals) was the key to expanding service in these communities. In their new facilities, these are true success stories.

Our Mendive and Gerlach sites are the only ones still operating close to their original plan. In Mendive's case (as mentioned above) the facility works well because it was designed to function effectively as a joint-use operation. Its good facilities and a cooperative staff relationship have allowed this library to flourish. In Gerlach's case, the facilities remain inadequate but the demand is so low for service (this desert community is located two hours north of Reno, with only 499 people counted in the 2000 U.S. Census) that minimal service is within acceptable limits.

Over the past decade and a half, Washoe County Library has been able to satisfy its commitment to reach underserved communities throughout the county by establishing school-public library partnerships. Overall, they have been an effective part of our plan to provide dynamic, service-oriented and cost-effective libraries to our public.

Building partnerships demands a commitment to individual excellence and to collaborative efforts. If there's a formula for success, it may revolve around your willingness to wrestle with these four "C" words: Collaborate, Communicate, Cooperate and Change. And if school-public partnerships sound like a good response to your service needs, we could add a fifth "C": it's time to find your partners and rise to the Challenge.

Public Library Joint-Use Partnerships: Challenges and Opportunities

Kathleen R. T. Imhoff

SUMMARY. With the growing emphasis on cooperation, collaboration and resource sharing, and increased competition for public resources, many educational institutions and public libraries are considering joint-use library facilities. This article explores the main types of partnership possibilities for academic institutions and public libraries in the United States and includes an in-depth outline of the challenges that face joint-use libraries. The article discusses methods of overcoming these challenges, opportunities, and advantages of partnering. A Feasibility Checklist for use in evaluating potential joint-use facilities is included as are sample contracts/agreements. *[Article copies available for a fee from The Haworth Document Delivery Service: 1-800-HAWORTH. E-mail address: <getinfo@haworth press.com> Website: <http://www.HaworthPress.com> © 2001 by The Haworth Press, Inc. All rights reserved.]*

Kathleen R. T. Imhoff is Associate Director, Bond Implementation Team, Broward County Library, the 9th largest public library, located in Fort Lauderdale, FL. A Graduate of the University of Wisconsin-Madison, she is a well-known lecturer, writer, workshop leader, technology innovator, and change agent. Having worked as an administrator in small rural libraries, a medium-sized library, a state library agency, and major urban libraries, she brings a unique perspective to joint-use partnering. She worked to formulate the guidelines for combined libraries in Wisconsin and helped establish and implement many of the Broward County Library partnerships. An active member of state, regional, national, and international library associations, she has served two terms as Councilor of the American Library Association, was a member and Chair of the John Cotton Dana Committee, President of the Public Relations Section, and twice President of the Public Library System Section of the Public Library Association.

[Haworth co-indexing entry note]: "Public Library Joint-Use Partnerships: Challenges and Opportunities." Imhoff, Kathleen R. T. Co-published simultaneously in *Resource Sharing & Information Networks* (The Haworth Information Press, an imprint of The Haworth Press, Inc.) Vol. 15, No. 1/2, 2001, pp. 17-39; and: *Joint-Use Libraries* (ed: William Miller, and Rita M. Pellen) The Haworth Information Press, an imprint of The Haworth Press, Inc., 2001, pp. 17-39. Single or multiple copies of this article are available for a fee from The Haworth Document Delivery Service [1-800-HAWORTH, 9:00 a.m. - 5:00 p.m. (EST). E-mail address: getinfo@haworthpress.com].

10.1300/J121v15n01_03

KEYWORDS. Joint-use facility, joint-use library, joint-use building, partnerships

INTRODUCTION

Because of a growing emphasis on cooperation and resource sharing, and the increased competition for public resources, many institutions are considering joint-use libraries. Public library board members, city and county officials, and academic administrators all search for creative partnerships and methods to stretch public dollars while providing a high level of public information and educational service. Privatization, outsourcing, and combined services are being explored by many agencies for services including school management, public library administration, and technology services. Joining academic and public libraries in formal partnerships also is being explored.

The joint-use concept has a number of antecedents. In the 1950s and 60s, many elementary and junior high schools provided public library service, with outside entrances in the school library for the public. They made a joint collection available to everyone in the community. However, as school populations continued to grow and resources for schools diminished, many of these libraries closed to the public. Now as land in urban areas becomes more scarce, many public libraries are looking for partners to share facilities in order to maximize space, avoid duplication of services, and maximize each institution's investment. In the 1990s with the birth of the charter school movement, these newly formed schools actively recruited educational partnerships with public libraries. Finally, as higher education institutions continue to provide additional, smaller satellite campuses, they, too, are looking to partner.

As the role of public libraries evolves into a higher level of teaching and providing information literacy, the goals of public libraries and academic institutions begin to converge. Cities are considering creating academic villages, land dedicated for the placement of all types of educational facilities: public schools from elementary through college or university, public libraries, museums, and other cultural facilities with educational components.

What Is a Joint-Use Library?

A joint-use library involves two or more libraries of different types coming together to provide services in a single building operating cooperatively to provide resources, such as curriculum support, bibliographic instruction, and information literacy to the general public and/or students, faculty, and administrators. In some cases, such as the case of a joint public and school library, the joint entity must meet the legal requirements. Some state laws do not provide a legal basis for such a combination. Check your state laws covering both types of libraries to ensure that a joint-use library establishment meets legal requirements. Depending on the state, accreditation agencies and/or the state library also need to be consulted so that the library meets accreditation requirements and state funding criteria, which criteria vary greatly from one state to the next. If a public library is involved, that fact also will mean providing the broader range of library services typically associated with public libraries to adults, youth and young children.

Partnership with a Public Library and an Elementary School

Several types of partnership possibilities exist with public libraries in the United States. The first type is between a school library and a public library. Although many of these elementary/public combined libraries were really just the school library opening its doors to the public, in the late 1970s there were several examples of purposely-built elementary school/public libraries. The library in Olney, Texas, which opened in 1973, is the best example of this type. Also, it is one of the longest-running school/public library combinations in the United States. The idea of a joint-use facility intrigues local governments. However, money-saving dreams quickly pale when examining the Olney Library, which is open sixty hours per week (four times more than the Fort Worth Main Branch), has three full-time and two part-time staff (double the full-time employees in other towns this size), and spends $30.86 per capita more than the North Texas average. All participating agencies feel that it is money well spent. All segments of the community use the building throughout the day even if there are school classes being held ("Working Together," 63). The physical layout of the space allows for easy separation of the materials for young children, and a separate area for class study. I have interviewed this staff at the Olney library twice over a twenty-year span, once in 1975 and once in 1998, and it is clear that the staff has a "can-do" attitude and 100% commitment to the concept of a joint-use library.

Major challenges to this type of combination are providing adequate security for the elementary school students, and isolating the adult materials from young children without providing artificial barriers. With the ever-growing concerns for student security, careful attention needs to be paid to all aspects of this critical matter.

Partnership with a Public Library and a Middle School

Public libraries also partner with middle school libraries. The Pembroke Pines Walter C. Young Library in Pembroke Pines, Florida is an example of this type of partnership. Security of the campus and collection access are challenges in this type of library also. The same pranks that middle school children do in schools, they do in joint libraries. Control of the children is particularly a problem before and after school and during lunch periods. Staff who work in this type of partnership library need to be very child-friendly and patient because of the high volume of students in the library both before and after school. A disadvantage can be the large number of children in the library at certain times, particularly after school. Their unabridged enthusiasm can create a high noise level. Public library patrons have learned to avoid using the library during this time period if they are bothered by the noise.

One advantage of this type of partnership is that locating within a school site brings high visibility. Many parents or caregivers drive or walk their children to school, bringing them daily into close proximity with the library. Conveniently scheduled after school programs provide opportunities for adults and children to use the library together. Many parents bring the students' younger siblings with them to select books for the entire family. Another advantage is the frequency of the student visits to the library. Many teachers schedule library time daily or weekly. This frequency allows the students to become familiar with the staff and build relationships with them. The joint use library in Pembroke Pines has a higher than average attendance at its summer school programs. So there is some evidence that the children are viewing the library as "the place to be" in the summer.

Partnership with a Public Library and a High School

A third possible partner for a public library is a public high school. The security and collection access issues are not as great with high school students, although they still need to be considered. Parking becomes a problem with a high school/joint partner library. People with special needs, young children, and elderly adults all need convenient easy parking to a public library. With so many high school students driving to school, the parking lot of this type of facility must be carefully planned, perhaps even fenced separately so that non-student library users will find adequate parking.

In smaller towns, usually those with fewer than 5,000 people, elementary, middle and high school functions are often combined in one complex of buildings. This complex often includes only one library/media center. Florence and Kohler, Wisconsin, are two cities with this type of combined service. In Florence the County Library Board and the School Board have a cooperative agreement to provide public library services in the elementary/high school library. There are separate school and library staffs who report to different administrations, do separate collection development, and have separate hours. In Kohler the joint-library is in the Kohler Area School District Building. This building is the site of the elementary, middle and high school. The library services are shared and both students and the general public can use the library during its convenient hours, which include the school day and Sunday afternoons.

Partnership with a Public Library and a Charter School

A variant on the high school partnership for public libraries is with a charter school. With the continued growth of the charter school movement, many charter schools are actively searching for partners. Many operate on a shoestring budget, and welcome other organizations to help them meet their service goals. One of the largest partnerships of this category is the Northwest Regional Library of the Broward County Library, partnering with the City of Coral Springs charter school.

For many years the public library had tried unsuccessfully to obtain property for a branch at a major intersection in densely populated Coral Springs. Suitable land was not available or well outside the County's budget until the city was able to buy an old shopping center on a prime intersection and locate a charter school there. Through skillful negotiation, both the library system and the city were able to reach their goals with a joint project of a 100,000 sf regional public library located on the charter high school site. The high school has about a thousand students. Each facility has a separate parking lot and a separate entrance. Security has been a major problem as many students use the library as a prank hangout. Additional security guards as well as off-duty police were necessary for this library to function.

Partnership with a Public Library and a Community or Junior College

The fifth type of partnership for a public library is one with a community or junior college. This type of partnership can be very successful since many public library collections are at a 2-year college level. Since most of the students are over the age of 18, the issues of access to the collection are eliminated. Also, community colleges have fairly open campuses with few campus security barriers. Parking can still be a problem. Some joint junior college/public libraries have library-card-only access to their parking lots. Broward County Library has operated a joint community college/public library since 1984 and has opened three more since then. One of these libraries has been the highest circulating library of the thirty-seven Broward County Libraries since the day it opened.

Partnership with a Public Library and a College or University

The final type of partnership for a public library is with a public college or university. There are different ways to form these partnerships. Library service for students can be contracted for with a public library located near a college campus so that the academic institution does not have to invest in building a separate library. Contractually, the collection money would go to the public library to provide curriculum support, a reserve room functions and faculty loan periods. Florida Atlantic University and the Broward County Library have had such a contract for services since 1985. The Florida legislature appropriated funds for Broward County Library to purchase resources for the university programs planned for the FAU downtown campus. Early funding was at a level to support new programs and books and serials to build Broward County Library's collection to a level supporting university curricular needs.

The San Jose Public Library and San Jose State University are joining together to form a landmark type of partnership. For the first time in the United States, a major urban main public library and a large state university library will be combined totally in one new building. Also, for the first time in the United States, a major urban county has formed a joint partnership with a private university to build a joint library facility. These two entities are Broward County Board of County Commissioners and Nova Southeastern University, which have come together to build the Nova Southeastern University Library, Research, and Information Technology Center. These two joint-use facilities are discussed in detail later in this collection.

Contracting for Services Partnership

In some instances when a public library exists and a new educational institution is created and needs library resources, instead of forming a joint library, the institution can contract with the public library to provide materials for its students. This arrangement works best with institutions that are within walking distances of each other. A yearly sum is determined for use and is applied toward the purchase of academic resources. The Broward County Main Library in downtown Fort Lauderdale is an example of this type of partnership serving as the library for the Florida Atlantic University downtown campus.

Advantages of Joint-Use Libraries

Many administrators begin looking at combining libraries as a way of saving money, thinking that they will be able to get a good library for half the dollars. However, while joint-use libraries do maximize resources, and do deliver more, they do not cost less money. When investigating a potential partnership it is important to realize up front that it will not be cheaper, but together you will be able to provide more resources to each constituent's base than if you worked separately. Purchasing power is increased to buy collections. Collections can be more diverse when you avoid the duplication of materials that would occur if you both had to buy the same book for two separate collections.

One of the partners may have a building site that ordinarily would not have been available to the other partner. In urban, built-out communities this is a real benefit. Many cities and schools bought land 20-30 years ago to hold for future development. Siting a joint-use facility on this well-placed land can benefit the entire community.

Communities like joint-use facilities. They perceive that their tax dollars are being well spent when they observe public agencies working together to avoid duplication. Although Nova Southeastern Library, Research and Information Technology Center is located in the heart of the Nova campus with only paid parking, more than 50% of all items circulated were checked out by the general public ("Nova Southeastern"). With a joint-use library the community gains a more in-depth collection when the partner is a college or university. These libraries also offer frequent computer and information literacy classes that might not have been available without a partnership.

Another advantage of a joint-use library is that it is an aid to recruitment of librarians. Often, when students graduate from library school they are uncertain about the type of library in which they would like to work. Being able to offer more than one type of library population to new recruits is a definite advantage. Also, if they are willing to transfer throughout the library departments they could experience services to youth, students, seniors, researchers and special use clientele all within the same building.

Goals for Partnering

According to Marshall Keyes at an address given at the 1994 SOLINET Annual meeting there are four goals to a partnership:

1. Be clear about the objectives of the partnership;
2. Choose partners that lead to strength;
3. Avoid illusions about partnerships; and
4. Remember that, unlike partnerships in the past, partnerships now are likely to be temporary.

All of the above goals should be considered when thinking about joint-use libraries. The benefits of a joint-use library usually far outweigh what one library can do by itself.

How Do Most Joint-Use Partnerships Come About?

In talking with libraries that have formed partnerships, these libraries have similar characteristics. They are likely to be part of several cooperatives or multi-type consortiums and to have had a long history of other cooperative efforts and projects. In most cases partnerships have been between people who knew each other, often beginning with casual conversation and a handshake. Concise guidelines about how to start a partnership which could lead to a joint-use facility can be found in the following books and articles: *How to Start a Partnership Library, Combined School and Public Libraries: A Guide for Decision Making*, and *The Librarian's Guide to Partnerships*.

What Are the Challenges That Joint-Use Libraries Face?

Although each partnership is unique, most joint-use libraries face the same challenges in the following areas:

1. Planning
2. Governance
3. Administration and Financing
4. Access to Information and Materials
5. The Physical Facility

6. Technology Integration
7. Attitudinal factors
8. Staffing
9. Identity

If the joint facility is new and built to serve as a joint-use library, the challenges are not as difficult. When one or both of the libraries already exist and they are trying to merge, those situations are more problematic. Both situations, through careful planning, can produce a successful partnership library.

Planning for a Joint-Use Library

It is important to examine the mission statements for both the public library and the partner library. In some places they will coincide. In others they will differ. The same will be true of each library's and governing body's long-range strategic plans. Have any studies been done to determine if a joint-use facility is the best alternative for the community? A thorough review of alternatives should also be carried out. Legal documents such as school charters, jurisdictional boundaries, establishing ordinances and laws governing both types of libraries need careful scrutiny. Discussion with and a site visit to any other joint-use libraries in your state would be beneficial. That staff could highlight challenges they faced and how they overcame them within the legal framework of your state. Early into the investigation process, it would be helpful to examine contracts of joint-use libraries in your state.

During the planning stage it is appropriate to involve concerned groups such as Friends of the Library, Foundations, school boards, public library boards, neighborhood associations, the funding entities for both libraries, and academic board of trustees. With a professional librarian's guidance, these groups should look at the complementary roles of a public library and its potential partner and the range of services necessary to meet these needs.

It is important to have a partner that you can trust. What is your partner's track record with previous cooperative projects? If it is a member of a multi-type cooperative or consortium and has a long history of successfully working with other libraries, the proposed joint facility has a higher chance of success. Early in the planning stage, staff of both libraries must meet frequently to help chart their joint course.

In this process each agency's goals must be explored to determine if there is enough common ground. You must pre-determine a point in the investigation when it is okay for either party to say, "No thanks." Also, it is critical to establish a point at which you re-confirm that you are going ahead and decide not to turn back. If these points are decided up front, there is less chance for misunderstanding and hard feelings if the investigation indicates that a joint-use library is not in everyone's best interest.

Governance of a Joint-Use Public/Academic Library

Governance includes determining how decisions will be made and who has the decision-making authority. Determining the type of governing structure is the most important factor in determining whether or not a joint-use facility will be successful. There are three main ways a joint facility can be governed.

1. The academic institution could govern the entire program. It could hire the staff, purchase materials, and administer everything through its regular channels, with a service agreement with the public library. The Nova Southeastern/Broward County Library is an example of this type of administrative structure.
2. The public library could govern the entire library through a service agreement with the academic institution. Broward County North Regional/Broward Community College Library is an example of this administrative model.
3. The public library and academic library could have two shared administrations housed together with some functions co-managed and others administrated separately by their individual unit. The new San Jose Library typifies this structure. This model is the most challenging.

In Broward County, Florida the public library governs five of the joint-use projects because that meets the needs of the two partners involved. Whatever governing structure is selected must be in accordance with prevailing state laws and local ordinances. Required functions not typically found in a public library but required in an academic library must be included in the joint-use plan. These functions might vary from library to library but could include items such as a quiet study room, computer labs, and a reserve room. There must be appropriate staff for the joint-use library to meet the state requirements for each type of library. The governing agreement or contract must include methods for conflict and grievance resolution, dissolution procedures, and a method for asset distribution if dissolved.

Administration and Financing

Administrative staff and frontline managers as well as the library directors must be involved in the establishment of the policies and procedures for the new library. If the staff is large enough to accommodate it, working groups should be created to explore and make recommendations on items such as user rights and responsibilities, hours of operation, circulation procedures, reference protocol, access to resources and activities, level of bibliographic instruction, and daily decision-making authority. Reciprocal borrowing, interlibrary loan, registration, and cataloging procedures deserve special attention.

A frequent stumbling block to co-managed joint-use library success is the difference in the terms and conditions of employment of the staff from each library. School employees are frequently nine-month employees while public staff typically works year round. Often, there are differences in the salary levels and benefit packages of each group. Unless some equitability can be achieved, these factors will be divisive issues among staff in a joint-use facility and could potentially lead to staff friction. A way to help alleviate this, if the salaries and benefits cannot be brought into line with each other, is to clearly state what each salary and benefits package is, and let the staff select the organization and position. If any of the existing employees are in bargaining units, the contracts must be carefully reviewed in order to be in compliance.

There are many different ways to finance a joint-use library. There is no right way or wrong way. You should examine the mechanisms used by joint-use libraries in your state or region and determine if any of those methods would work in your situation. There are three items to consider in funding a joint-use library: initial building costs, on-going operational and maintenance costs, and future capital costs. If the building is located on a school campus, the school might find it more cost effective to provide the grounds care, janitorial cleaning and building security, even if the public library provides all the other operating costs under contract. Initial and on-going funding of the project is extremely important, but since funding is a uniquely local issue, you need to work this through with your local funding agencies.

Access to Information and Materials

Joint-use libraries have taken many different approaches to collection access and collection building. Depending on local community standards, some joint facilities have separate areas of the collection for certain age groups. This separation is most prevalent in partnerships with elementary, middle school and high school libraries. Melding the collection as much as possible makes for truly integrated resources and better use of the collection. In some instances, there are representatives from both types of libraries responsible for collection building. Other times, the school staff submit suggestions to the public library staff for their purchase consideration. In another model of joint collection development, a committee selects the materials.

Policies and procedures need to be jointly established for dealing with challenges to materials or Internet sites by parents, faculty and citizens. A clear, well-supported policy on Internet access is an integral part of a successful joint-use library. The building should be designed to place children's computers separate from those used by adults. The Internet Access Policy must be consistent with the mission statement of both the school and public library.

The operating schedule must work well for both agencies. Compromises might have to be made to accommodate the needs of college students for early and late hours. The Nova Southeastern Library is open 100 hours per week starting at 7:30 a.m. and closing at midnight. However, the Children's Department closes at 9:00 p.m.

The Physical Facility

Buildings that are specifically built for a joint-use facility are those that function best. Many communities consider a joint-use facility when they have an old unused building they own. Older buildings with many load-bearing walls could inhibit successful joint-use. Many administrators still think it is cheaper to renovate an old building than it is to build a new one, but in most areas of the country, it costs at least 85% of the cost of new construction to renovate an old building. In addition to the high cost of renovation, old buildings usually require very costly changes to make the building ADA compliant.

Often, the school library is situated in the center of the school complex for the convenience of the students and faculty and is connected to the classrooms with walking paths. Most of the public will be driving to the library and should be able to park within 200-500 feet from the library entrance. There must be a convenient outside entrance for the public if the joint-use facility is located in a school building. Another factor to be addressed is an arrangement within the school building so the library facility including rest rooms and meeting rooms can be

opened during the evenings, summers, and weekend hours without
jeopardizing building security.

Technological Integration

If the partnership is between two new libraries or one new and one
old library, the choices of equipment, software, networking and automation systems are not too difficult. However, when two existing libraries come to the joint-use planning table with separate automation
vendors, each group of staff is emotionally attached to its existing vendor. It is critical in this situation for each group to determine what is essential and come to the table with an open mind and the willingness to
jointly make a decision in a timely manner. San Jose is an example of a
joint-use situation where each library previously had a different type of
computer system. After the technology planning team determined what
was key to both libraries, they actively searched throughout the United
States to determine what would work for the new joint-use library. Not
only did this process result in a new vendor being selected, but it also
brought staff from the public and academic libraries together working
for a common goal.

Attitudinal Factors

A "can do" attitude is the single most important factor in forming a
successful joint-use library. For over 25 years, the Broward County Library has believed that all partnerships strengthen and expand the resources available to the patrons. Sometimes, when the decision to create
a new joint library is announced, staff, students, administrators, faculty
and the general public bring to the forefront reasons why that particular
partnership won't work. They include misconceptions like: there will
be hordes of crying babies and doddering, old people in "my" library,
public librarians don't know how to answer "academic" research questions, homeless people will be roaming the school campus if it is open to
the public, and the school children will be checking out all the "dirty"
books. While all of these could be problems, "can-do" advocates of the
joint-use library can help change this negative thinking.

Many times the joint-use deal is very high profile. In San Jose, the
Mayor and the University President were the individuals who made the
decision to go ahead with their large joint project. Nova Southeastern
University worked directly with the Broward County Board of Commissioners to create their joint-use agreement. Negative attitudes, mis-

trust, and rumors must be overcome with a "can-do" attitude to improve the chances of the joint-use library succeeding. Improving service rather than meeting political objectives or saving money must be the overriding concern in establishing a joint-use library. The decision makers and other key individuals must be genuinely enthusiastic about the project and dedicated to making it work despite potential conflicts and difficulties. In all successful joint-use partnerships there is at least one key individual who is passionate about the project and will not take "no" for an answer. This leader's attitude and vision then energize the other project staff.

In joint-use projects that were not so successful or dissolved, usually administrators created them with no input or buy-in from the staff that had to implement the project. The mixing of senior adults, preschoolers, teenagers and the homeless needs to be viewed as non-threatening by the staff, by potential users, and by the responsible agencies. According to the people in Olney, Texas (population of 4,600), which has a twenty-nine year history of a well-used joint school public library, it helps if the community is a "cooperative community" ("Working Together," 64). If you have a town or a city with political problems, it is more difficult to introduce a joint project, to see it through, and to sustain it.

Staff

Committed and flexible staff is the key to achieving a hospitable, comfortable environment in a joint-use library. Along with commitment, the reporting structure and job duties must be clearly defined. San Jose chose to have many functions, such as reference, co-managed. However, the two entities worked for over a year to reach that decision and have outlined clearly everyone's duties and responsibilities. It is not possible to manage a joint building with the same number of staff of the single function library. Most towns the size of Olney, Texas would have a half-time librarian. The Olney Community Library and Arts Center has three full-time and two part-time staff for 60 open hours.

It is best to hire staff that is "cooperation ready." During recruitment interviews, ask questions about the candidate's philosophy of cooperation and try to determine openness to work with people of all ages comfortably. When possible, offer public service staff non-public service responsibilities if they are not comfortable with the changed patronage. The staff will be the people to greet and serve the users of the new joint facility. Work with them to view everyone who comes through the door as their customer. Help them catch the possibilities of a partnership library. As they identify things that could be improved through this new endeavor, be aware of the need for constant evaluation and revision to how things are done. Welcome their input into this process.

Identity

When two new libraries embark on a new joint-use library project, they create an identity, name, logo, and key messages. Because each had a clean slate, this process is fairly easy. However, when one or both entities existed prior to the partnership, identity issues can be a tricky maze. There is a melding of cultures, not just institutions. In a joint-use facility two important agencies are coming together to cooperate. Both of the funding sources for those agencies want and deserve adequate credit for their contributions to the partnership. If recognition is done to the satisfaction of each party, this will be another ingredient in a winning partnership.

Once the new identity has been established, which should be as early into the process as possible, a clear plan needs to be developed for the transition to the new name/logo including all printed materials and building signs. Issues surrounding how the collection is identified and whether or not it is to be relabeled need to be part of that plan. Some recognizable identity from each institution should be retained. In some cases, a totally new name is selected to identify the new joint-use library. This is the case with San Jose, where the San Jose Public Library and the San Jose State University Library merged into the new Clark Library. They are actively transitioning to the use of this name for their new library, which will open in 2003.

Naming can be a very sensitive issue and the discussions leading up to decision-making must be handled with great care to avoid hard feelings, which are difficult to soothe later. The earlier the process of choosing a name and identity starts, the easier it will be. Also, it is wise to have decided these issues before a formal agreement is signed so the new name can be in the original documents. Saving this decision until right before the building is opened will not make it an easier one.

How Do You Decide If a Joint Library Will Work?

After all nine areas have been explored in depth, use the following checklist to help analyze your process and decision. Then you should determine which areas need more work and study. It might be helpful before the checklist is filled out to agree jointly which of the fifty-five items are critical if you are to have a satisfactory partnership. Identify what a successful partnership will look like. The required items will vary between projects.

FEASIBILITY CHECKLIST

This checklist will help libraries and communities decide whether separate school and public libraries, a joint school and public library, or some other alternative will offer the best library services in their particular locality. In this checklist I use the word "school" library to mean any type of school library from elementary to university library.

Planning

1. Mission statements for the public library and the school library are clearly understood and supported by all parties. There is an understanding of how these missions coincide, how they differ, and how they will be carried out.
2. There is knowledge of any existing planning documents for the public library and school library programs, and agreement on how these documents can be integrated and priorities established.
3. A study of the feasibility and suitability of the joint library facility has been conducted, including a review of alternatives to a joint-use library.
4. Concerned groups have examined carefully the complementary role of the school and public libraries and are aware of the range of services and resources which must be offered to meet the needs of both user populations. (Examples of concerned groups include: Friends of the Library, Foundation, School Board, Public Library Board, City or Town Council, and Academic Board of Trustees.)
5. Community members or neighborhood associations are involved in and support the decision to have a combined school and public library program.
6. The jurisdictional boundaries of the school service area and the public library area are similar.

7. The two agencies involved in the joint program have defined their responsibilities in a draft formal agreement drawn up during the planning phase.
8. The issue of dissolving the joint facility has been discussed and all parties agree on how assets would be divided.

Governance

Public Library

9. The public library program will be established in accordance with state and local laws.
10. If required, a legally appointed and constituted public library board will govern the operation of the public library program.

School Library

11. The school library program will be established in accordance with state and local laws and regulations.
12. If required, appropriately licensed/certified library media personnel provide curriculum services to the school library program in accordance with the provisions stated in the regulating code, ordinances or laws.
13. School related services will be provided such as reserve room functions or quiet study areas.

Joint Library

14. It has been agreed upon which agency will govern the library.
15. This agreement has been formally approved by each governing agency.
16. A simple procedural method has been determined to deal with conflict and/or grievances.
17. Sharply defined policies and procedures are set forth for hiring, evaluating and dismissing library staff.

Administration and Financing

18. General policies and procedures for operating the joint library have been discussed and all parties agree on principal elements, i.e., hours of operation, access to resources and activities, users rights and responsibilities, and authority for daily decision-making.

19. The reciprocal borrower's privileges and interlibrary loan policies of each library will be continued.
20. The governing agency will follow statutory requirements as to fiscal year audits, budgeting process, and annual reports to the municipal governing authority for the public library and the authority for the school library.
21. The salaries and benefits of all employees will be similar, based on comparable qualifications and job expectations.
22. If both nine and twelve month employees are staff, equitable arrangements have been worked out and agreed upon.
23. If any of the employees of existing libraries are in bargaining units, all contractual agreements have been met.
24. Maintenance and security arrangements have been made.
25. If any functions are to remain separate or policies distinct, they have been clearly delineated and supported by all parties.
26. A clear, written understanding of the initial financing of the joint-use facility has been agreed upon by all funding bodies.

Access to Information and Materials

27. The library will be open to the public the recommended number of hours for its population group according to state or local standards.
28. A collection development policy consistent with the mission statements has been developed to guide selection of materials in all formats for both school and public library clientele.
29. The issue of access to material for all age groups and maturity level has been discussed in detail and is thoroughly understood by all parties, including potentially controversial adult materials.
30. An Internet Access Policy consistent with the mission statements of the school and public library has been developed and is supported by all parties.
31. Staff responsibility for selection of materials has been clearly assigned.

The Physical Facility

32. The joint-use building is in compliance with the provisions of Title II of the Americans with Disabilities Act (ADA).
33. The building is easily accessible to the public, to students, and faculty. There is an entrance directly into the library from the outside at ground floor (entry at grade without steps or ramp).

34. The building design permits nearby parking for library users (within 200-500 feet from the library entrance) as well as easy access to the library from the classrooms.
35. The building provides adequate space to implement the full range of library services consistent with each library's long-range plan, and state standards.
36. The building provides adequate public restroom facilities.
37. The library facility, including restrooms and meeting rooms, can be opened during the evenings, summers, and weekend hours without jeopardizing building security.
38. In an elementary, middle or high school joint-use library, an area is provided for adult materials not easily accessible to minors but openly accessible to the public.

Technology Integration

39. There is agreement on how equipment, software and other aspects of technology will be purchased or licensed and how access will be provided to students, faculty, and the public.
40. There is agreement on the vendor for the automated circulation system.

Staffing

41. All staff are committed to the philosophy of a joint-use library.
42. The staff reporting structure is clearly outlined and job duties defined.
43. There are adequate staff to cover all the functions of both libraries.
44. Previously existing staff have accepted changes to their previous duties.
45. If any functions are co-managed, ultimate responsibility is defined.

Attitudinal Factors

46. Improving service, rather than saving money, is the overriding element in planning a joint-use library.
47. Decision makers and key individuals (administrators and employees) are genuinely enthusiastic about the project and dedicated to making it work, despite potential difficulties.
48. The concerned community groups realize that a joint-use program is not necessarily a more economical means of offering li-

brary services to both students and community members than separate facilities for school and public programs would be.

49. All adults, not only parents of students, will feel comfortable and welcome on the site of the joint-use library.
50. The mixing of preschoolers, children, teenagers, and senior adults is seen not as threatening or uncomfortable by any of the potential users or the responsible agencies.
51. The combined library provides the best opportunity for your community to obtain the following:

    a. Professional library personnel with a specialization in school librarianship.
    b. Professional library personnel with a specialization in public librarianship.
    c. A means for strengthening the material resources available to the users.
    d. An adequately planned program of services to meet the needs of both public and school-based users.

Identity

52. A mutually acceptable name and logo have been selected for the new facility and agreed upon by all of the concerned groups.
53. A determination has been made if any co-branding will be allowed.
54. A plan is in place to transition from the old names/logos to the new name/logo including all printed materials and building signs.
55. A means of identifying materials in the collection has been developed.

Contracts/Agreements

Once it has been determined that the joint project will come to fruition, both agencies need to begin working on a list of items for inclusion in the written, legal document. Each state and in some cases cities or counties have relevant statutory requirements that pertain to each type of library. Be certain to check with your appropriate state and local agencies so you know the applicable laws and regulations from the beginning rather than discovering later legal roadblocks that can't be overcome. Each agency has a significant investment that must be protected in the agreement.

The formal written document can be a contract or an agreement depending on local requirements. This document should cover the staffing, finances, physical building, ownership of all assets, terms and conditions of dissolution. It should not include the procedures of how the day-to-day activities will take place. Those procedures should be outlined in a memo of understanding or a jointly developed policy and procedure handbook approved by each party to the agreement. Other essential parts to the contract include the following items:

- The contract needs to be multi-year, if possible, due to the often complicated and time-consuming approval process of some academic institutions and municipalities.
- The contract needs to have an easy amendment process to accommodate the unknown. Each partnership is unique and it is impossible to anticipate every circumstance in the beginning.
- Rather than using fixed dollar amounts or percentages in the contract, which would require yearly changes as costs escalate, use general language, e.g., "The college will pay all maintenance costs" or "The public library will pay all costs associated with the staffing and benefits."

Because legal requirements vary greatly in each state and local jurisdiction, it is recommended highly that you consult your own institution's legal counsel.

CONCLUSION

Since Broward County Library formed its first academic/public library partnership in 1981, the number of Broward County Library's joint-use libraries has grown to seven, one with a middle school, two with charter high schools, four with community colleges, and one with a private university, as well as several contracts with adjacent universities to provide university library services within the Broward County Main Library. Each partnering occasion has been a learning experience for all involved. By joining together, each partner has improved the services available to all of the people of Broward county. The partnership with a private university, the first of its kind in the United States, opened the doors to the public for the first time to the over 400,000 items in the university's research-based collection.

What Is the Next Step?

Plan carefully; study all options for partnering to increase service. Look for partners you can trust and seek wholehearted commitment from all parties involved. With strong library partnerships, together you can transform tomorrow.

REFERENCES

Call, I. S. "Joint-Use Libraries: Just How Good Are They?" *College and Research Libraries News, v.* 54 (November, 1993), 551-2.

Combined School & Public Libraries; Guidelines for Decision Making. Wisconsin Department of Public Instruction, Division of Library Services. Madison, Wisconsin, 1994.

Conaway, Peggy. "One Reference Service for Everyone? Designing a Joint Service for San Jose Public Library and San Jose State University," *Library Journal* 125 no. 12 (July, 2000), 42-44.

Haycock, Ken. "Building the 21st Century Library; Schools and Public Libraries Working Together." February 2001. <http://institute21.stanford.edu/programs/workshop/facilities/schools_handout.pdf >, p. 8.

How to Start a Partnership Library, Washoe County Library System, Reno, Nevada, 1993.

Imhoff, Kathleen R. T. *Making the Most of New Technology; A How-To-Do-It Manual for Libraries,* New York: Neal Schuman, 1996.

Jaffe, Lawrence Lewis. "Collection Development and Resource Sharing in the Combined School/Public Library," *Collection Management,* v. 7, (Fall 1985-Winter 1986), 205-6.

Lynch, Sherry, editor. *The Librarian's Guide to Partnerships.* Highsmith Press, Fort Atkinson, Wisconsin: Highsmith, 1999.

"Nova Southeastern Library Usage Exceeds All Expectations," *Broward County Sun E-News,* Fort Lauderdale, Florida. Monday September 16, 2002.

Olson, Rene. "2 in 1: Designing a Combined Library that Works for Everybody," *School Library Journal, v.* 42 (February 1996), 24-7.

"Working Together: Twenty Years into 'the Olney Experiment,' Pioneer City/School Library Still Succeeds." *Texas Libraries,* v. 55 (Fall/Winter '94-'95), 63-5.

APPENDIX I. Joint-Use Libraries Summary

Possible Advantages	Possible Disadvantages
• Improved collection of resources	• Governance and management issues
• More services	• Fewer adults willing to use the "school" campus library
• Less duplication	• Crowded facility
• More computers	• Lengthy planning process
• Expanded hours of service	
• Better use of funds	
• Improved community image	

Common Problems
• Basic differences in purpose, resulting in role conflict
• Location of site and location within the site
• Loss of autonomy
• Restricted circulation of some items
• Intellectual freedom issues
• Inconvenient, inadequate parking
• Staff not committed to partnering
• Difference in staff benefits and salaries

Figure 1. Joint-use Library Advantages, Disadvantages, and Common Problems.
Source: Haycock, Ken. "Building the 21st Century Library, Schools and Public Libraries Working Together." February 2001.

Joint-Use Libraries:
The Broward Community College
Central Campus Experience

Julia A. Woods

SUMMARY. The University/College Library at Broward Community College Central Campus is a joint-use library serving the users of Broward Community College and Florida Atlantic University-Broward. This full service academic library has been in operation since 1994 in a new facility and with a joint governing board that includes all partners. The combination of resources by the partners has provided a workable solution to the problems of providing needed library services and access to materials for the users. There are advantages and disadvantages to such a solution which need to be understood and accepted by the partners as compromise and adjustments are necessary to make the whole a positive working solution. *[Article copies available for a fee from The Haworth Document Delivery Service: 1-800-HAWORTH. E-mail address: <getinfo@haworth press.com> Website: <http://www.HaworthPress.com> © 2001 by The Haworth Press, Inc. All rights reserved.]*

KEYWORDS. Joint-use library, Florida Atlantic University, Broward Community College

Julia A. Woods is Dean, University/College Library & Learning Resources, Broward Community College, 3501 SW Davie Road, Davie, FL 33314 (E-mail: jwoods@broward.edu).

[Haworth co-indexing entry note]: "Joint-Use Libraries: The Broward Community College Central Campus Experience." Woods, Julia A. Co-published simultaneously in *Resource Sharing & Information Networks* (The Haworth Information Press, an imprint of The Haworth Press, Inc.) Vol. 15, No. 1/2, 2001, pp. 41-53; and: *Joint-Use Libraries* (ed: William Miller, and Rita M. Pellen) The Haworth Information Press, an imprint of The Haworth Press, Inc., 2001, pp. 41-53. Single or multiple copies of this article are available for a fee from The Haworth Document Delivery Service [1-800-HAWORTH, 9:00 a.m. - 5:00 p.m. (EST). E-mail address: getinfo@haworthpress.com].

10.1300/J121v15n01_04

41

Interlibrary cooperation through the creation of joint-use libraries has been developing and operational in Broward County for several decades. In the early 1980s, Broward Community College and the Broward County Public Library System began a partnership that has continued to provide library services to community college students and community users. The first joint-use operation was established at the South Campus in 1983 when that partnership of a public community college and county library system was the first effort of its kind in Florida.[1] The accomplishments of that partnership led to a similar development on the North Campus of the College.

Because of campus-based management, the North and South Campuses of the College have separate but similar agreements with the County Library System. The buildings are owned by and located on College property and the College is responsible for the building and its maintenance while the County Library System is responsible for the operations of the library, its staffing and services. Included in the agreements are the number of titles to be purchased and the amount of funding to go into the collection of materials to support the community college programs. This pattern of community college and public library cooperation has been repeated at the Pines and Downtown Centers of the College. The exception to the public library/community college partnership is located on the BCC Central Campus.

THE CENTRAL CAMPUS EXPERIENCE

The Central Campus followed a different path in the development of its joint-use library. During the 1960s and 1970s, the people of Broward County expressed a desire to have a public university located in the County, and the political pressure resulted in action in the mid-1980s. The State University System directed Florida Atlantic University and Florida International University to offer programs and courses in the County. The two universities were selected to provide this service as they are located in the counties just north (FAU) and south (FIU) of Broward. The majority of courses were offered at the Central Campus of BCC in Davie, Florida while the administrative offices and some courses were located at the downtown Ft. Lauderdale site of BCC.

On the Central Campus, library personnel from the three institutions provided services from a small library facility that was shared with the Learning Resource Center. The personnel worked under the policies, rules and regulations of their home institutions. This practice was sustained for several years while both of the Universities were developing fast-growing programs in the County. In 1989, the State University System designated that Florida Atlantic University would be the lead public university in Broward County, and Florida International University would maintain a presence in the county and offer programs not duplicated by FAU. This resulted in a reduction in the programs provided by FIU but a continued need to provide library services to the students and faculty of that institution.

In the early 1990s, two circumstances coincided that resulted in the decision to build a joint library. The first was that the extensive growth of the university programs made FAU consider building a library facility on the BCC Central Campus. The second was that BCC recognized its current library facility was inadequate and that it needed to construct a larger library and learning resources building. The funding for the joint use building was provided to the Community College by the State Legislature, but when the program for the building was developed, additional money was needed. That additional funding was provided by the State University System with a smaller amount also being contributed by the State Department of Education which had an interest in developing joint library facilities.

The program for the building was a joint effort of a committee made up of employees from the three institutions. While the facility and land were owned by BCC, it was understood from the outset that it was a joint facility and there would be participation by all three organizations in the development of the building program and operations of the library.

During the same time period that the new facility was being designed and constructed, the administrations of BCC and FAU made the decision to hire a consultant to study issues relating to the governance and joint administration of the new library. The consultant, Alphonse F. Trezza, a senior faculty member of the School of Library and Information Science at Florida State University, was asked to do the following:

1. develop an organizational structure that would provide a clear delineation of responsibilities and duties for all employees . . . in the library;
2. develop an operational agreement for the joint-use facility to insure a smooth operation that would meet the needs of students, faculty, and staff at both institutions.[2]

In 1994, Dr. Trezza spent six months in discussions with administrators, librarians and faculty before presenting a report that was accepted by the Presidents of BCC and FAU. The major recommendations provided that there be the establishment of an integrated library, the merging of the two staffs under one library administration, the establishment of a governance/policy advisory committee, the potential financial obligations for three years, the setting up of a liaison librarian between FAU-Broward and BCC, and implementation procedures and a time-table.[3] With the acceptance of the report by the Presidents of BCC and FAU, the University/College Library at Broward Community College officially came into being.

An inter-institutional agreement covered the issues of governance, service and funding responsibilities. The decision was made to have the Director of the Library report to a governing board made up of representatives of the partners. The Provost of the Central Campus of BCC, with input of the Governing Board and the Vice-President of FAU-Broward, would evaluate the Director, who would be a BCC employee. The rest of the staff would be BCC employees but would serve both institutions.

A twelve-member governing board for the library was established and called the Governance/Policy Advisory Committee (GPAC). Voting members from the Broward Community College Central Campus are the Academic Dean, one department chair and two academic faculty members. Voting members from Florida Atlantic University-Broward are the Associate Vice President, the Director of the University Library (located on the FAU Main Campus), one administrative officer with faculty status, and one academic faculty member. Until the University moved its classes to another site, one representative from Florida International University served as a voting member on the Committee. Non-voting members of the Committee are the FAU Broward Library Liaison, the University/College Library Director, and, from the joint library staff, one library faculty and one career employee.

The governing board is responsible for reviewing the budget, long range planning, evaluation of user services, and any other major policy matters. After GPAC reviews and approves the annual budget proposal, the Director presents it to the Provost of the BCC Central Campus and the Vice-President of FAU-Broward. GPAC serves as the search committee for the position of the Director of the Library and is to be an advocate for the library. The Chair of the GPAC revolves on an annual basis between FAU and BCC.

Another responsibility of the governing committee is the establishment of standing committees which include the Budget Committee, a Bylaws Committee and the Library/Learning Resources Advisory Committee. These committees continue to function with the most active being the Library/Learning Resources Advisory Committee. The Learning Resources Center became a part of the Advisory Committee as a result of FAU contracting with BCC for audio-visual services on the Central Campus.

The Library/Learning Resources Advisory Committee includes three faculty representatives from BCC, three faculty representatives from FAU and one student representative from both FAU and BCC. One FIU faculty representative served on that committee until the University moved its classes to another site. The Directors of the Library and the Learning Resources Center served as ex-officio members until the two departments combined into one administrative unit. Since that reorganization, the Dean of Libraries and Learning Resources and the Director of Learning Resources serve as ex-officio members. The responsibilities of the Committee include advising on issues of collection development, quality of user services and proposed changes in services. A change is taking place as a result of FAU employees assuming the responsibility for the delivery of audio-visual services to the institution. At that point the committee became the Library Advisory Committee while retaining the same membership and responsibilities.

The Trezza Report included recommendations on funding responsibilities. After looking at the student population, the recommendation for funding distribution went as follows: BCC-60%, FAU-35% and FIU-5%. This recommendation was accepted in theory with the results being that BCC did contribute 60% and FAU contributed 40%. Until it left the Central Campus, FIU made a $50,000 annual contribution that was part of the FAU assessment. It was also recommended that this be a minimum contribution and that it would be to the benefit of each institution to build on this base in order to help the library fulfill its mission.

The Trezza Report included a recommendation that staff in the U/C Library be under the personnel administration of Broward Community College where librarians had faculty status and would be covered by BCC's salary scale and benefits package. The employees of the FAU Library who had been working at the site were offered the option of joining the integrated U/C Library staff or being provided positions elsewhere in the FAU Library system. One of the FAU staff members opted to join the U/C Library staff. As there had been problems between the staff members, the Trezza Report recommended the following:

> The consultant feels very strongly, . . . , that a split of staff between FAU-Broward and BCC will not be effective. The present arrangement strongly indicates the conflict between the two staffs. I

know of no joint arrangement where the staff is divided and reports to two administrators that works effectively. I cannot, in my
professional judgment, recommend anything but a fully integrated
library, staff and services.[4]

Collection Development concerns were addressed with the recommendation to develop one policy for the library. The first integrated policy was
created by the GPAC and was approved by that group and future revisions
and policies have been approved by the Library Advisory Committee.

The decision was made that the circulation and online catalog databases for the library would be maintained in the statewide Community
College System. The small FAU-Broward collection was loaded into that
database while the U/C Library also maintained one terminal that connected to FAU which was a part of the State University System library
automation system. This provided access to the information needed to
validate FAU patrons. In subsequent years, it has been possible to have
both the BCC and FAU networks available in the joint library, thereby
providing access to an array of information and resources for authorized
users. It has also enabled an FAU student to have the same access to information that would be available to a student at the Main Campus.

The first Director of the University/College Library was employed in
July of 1995. The first year under the agreement had been finished and
the first phase of the new building was almost completed. The library and
learning resources were moved into the new building for the 1995/96 academic year while the old part of the facility was renovated and the final
move into the completed facility took place in the summer of 1996.

DEVELOPMENT OF THE U/C LIBRARY

While not all recommendations from the Trezza report were implemented, the majority were adopted and have been very workable. The
model of one integrated library with a Governing Board and Library
Advisory Committee made up of representatives of all the participants
has provided opportunities for input into the operations and services by
all participants. The extra efforts necessary to keep all partners informed and participating has provided a support that has made it possible for the library to grow and provide necessary services.

The creation of one collection development policy for the Library
has provided the opportunity for selection of materials by the faculty
and library staff members who are familiar with the curriculum being
taught on the Campus. There has been one major expansion of the docu-

ment, and that policy has continued to provide the basis for a growing collection. Collection development has been especially challenging due to the rapid growth of an additional seven university programs that were added to the curriculum in a three year period. The funding for the new programs came from the regular resource budget for all programs and was initially very limited. In subsequent years overall resource funding has increased the upper level and graduate print collection but FAU students have needed additional support. That support has come in the form of access to electronic databases from the main FAU library and an active use of the U/C Library Interlibrary Loan Department.

The funding formula has not needed to be changed, and with a variance of a few points for several years, has remained BCC 60% and FAU 40%. The growth of the overall budget has been substantial and reflects an increase of just over 60% since 1995. It has also been very helpful that all of the partners have been able to provide additional funding for expense and capital items beyond the base formula.

Surveys by FAU and BCC have indicated that students are satisfied with the services and collections provided by the U/C Library. Responding to the results of a student survey, the hours of the library were recently extended to 89 1/2 hours per week. Survey results also indicate that there is satisfaction with the materials provided in the print collection which has gone from 148,381 to 218,682 volumes. There is no question that there is an increase in the resources available to students as a result of the partnership.

Having a Director report to a governing board and the administrator of one of the partners could provide problems but has not done so to this point. Credit for making this structure work goes to the administrators of the partnership who understand that accommodations and compromises are necessary to make the partnership work.

ADVANTAGES AND DISADVANTAGES

Given the fact that it can be more complicated to put together and maintain operations of a joint-use library, why try at all? The obvious and most important advantage to this type of cooperative venture is the pooling of resources to meet the needs of the institutions. The shrinking resources and increasing needs faced by many institutions require creative solutions to accomplish desired goals. By combining resources, the institutions may be able to increase the quantity of collections, the quality of services or the building of facilities that could not have been accomplished by a single agency.

The pooling of resources can provide a synergy that is reflected in more than the tangible outcomes of a building, a larger collection or more staff. It is also reflected in the interactions that can take place between the staffs of the organizations that can result in new ideas for services or methods of operation. Field trips by staff to the two libraries have resulted in an exchange of ideas and information that has been beneficial in the development of new policies and procedures for the U/C Library. Changes in ILL operations were a result of a meeting of staff members from both libraries that resulted in a streamlining of operations. Sharing information about the collection, use of equipment, services such as photocopy or print recovery vendors, database training and other administrative operations have been very useful. The combining of energy from the partners can be useful in developing a whole that is bigger than its parts.

A disadvantage that can come from this type of cooperative venture is the loss of control by one institution. While some would consider this a disadvantage, it does not outweigh the results obtained by the pooling of resources. However, it is a facet of a cooperative venture that needs to be recognized. The human species can be very territorial and the need to "have our own" and the fear that "they will take over" will be out there. Even when the participants recognize that they are getting "more bang for the buck" by cooperating, there is a desire to maintain a level of control that can result in a tension between the partners. The need to compromise and adjust to meet the needs of all partners is not an easy task but can be done when the partners come to the table with the will to make the cooperative venture successful. The willingness to compromise can be enhanced when it is clear that the joint venture has the support of the administrations of the partners.

There is another aspect of working in a cooperative venture that needs to be addressed. It is not an advantage or disadvantage, but it must be recognized that the education process that goes on between the library, its governing administration and its users is extended to the number of partners participating in the joint venture. Additional time and effort in the education process can be extensive. The Library is not communicating with one group but with all partners and making sure that information is fairly and continuously shared is important. Meetings take place with the students, faculty and staff of all partners with minor adjustments in the message that apply to the particular partners' needs. Explaining to a faculty member or student the difference between what the joint library provides and what is available to them from the home library is an on-going process. For example, extra time is needed to explain to BCC students why they cannot have access to proprietary databases on the FAU network even though that network is in the U/C Library. Extra time is needed to communicate to FAU students about why they need to reactivate their library card each semester instead of once a year as they do on the Main Campus. Communication is important so that the users understand what options they have available from all their libraries.

Another aspect to be addressed when working in a cooperative venture is historical loyalties. Unless the joint library is in a position to hire all new people, the staff can have a tendency to maintain old loyalties at the expense of the new partners. Effort will be needed to help staff embrace the users of the new partners. Increasing outreach to the faculty, student and staff of the partners provides the library staff with the opportunity to become familiar with the needs of the partners. It also provides the faculty and staff of the new partner with the opportunity to become familiar with available services and a venue to express the needs it would like to have met.

RECOMMENDATIONS

Institutions that are interested in going into a cooperative venture to develop a joint-use library should consider the following:

1. Involvement of the major players or the representatives of all partners in the planning process. More heads provide more input, information, and buy-in.
2. Support of the top administrators of the partners is very important to the success of a joint-use library.
3. The responsibilities of the partners need to be as clearly defined as possible before the endeavor begins. Those responsibilities can change or expand with time but the understanding of what the responsibilities are should be outlined in a written agreement or contract.
4. Compromise on the part of all partners will be required to make the cooperative venture successful.
5. The Library needs to provide the leadership required to work out compromises and to establish the new procedures and processes for successful services. There will be a level of uncertainty on the part of the participants, especially at the beginning of the project, but in time the level of uncertainty will be reduced by the provision of effective services.

Joint-use libraries can be a workable solution to the problem of the decreasing resources facing many institutions. By combining resources the partners are able to provide more for their users but in doing so they will be losing some control. Compromise is necessary from the partners for the whole to be successful.

REFERENCES

1. I.S. (Bud) Call. "Joint-Use Libraries: Just How Good Are They." *College & Research Libraries*, 10 (November 1993) 551-552.
2. Alphonse F. Trezza. "Organizational Structure and Operational Agreement for A Joint Use Facility" for Broward Community College and Florida Atlantic University-Broward, Davie, Florida, a Study and Recommendations. June 23, 1994.
3. Trezza.
4. Trezza 28.

APPENDIX

EXECUTIVE SUMMARY

ORGANIZATIONAL STRUCTURE AND OPERATIONAL AGREEMENT FOR A JOINT USE FACILITY for Broward Community College and Florida Atlantic University-Broward, Davie, Florida, a Study and Recommendations, Prepared by Alphonse F. Trezza, Consultant, June 23, 1994.

The basic elements for providing effective and timely service to meet the needs of the faculty, students and staff of Florida Atlantic-Broward, Florida International-Broward, and Broward Community College are first, a single integrated library service with one staff, one collection, and one budget. This integrated library, referred to hereafter as the University/College Library (UCL) will need strong budgetary support, a qualified and service-oriented staff, and library resources strong in quality and sufficient in quantity to support the academic programs. In addition, computers and other technologies, with the availability of academic databases, and participation in the major networking consortia and operations, are essential to support the present and future expanding and developing academic programs. It is important to recognize the consultant's assumption, confirmed in meetings with the Presidents of FAU and BCC that this academic library is designed to serve four-year undergraduate programs and masters degree programs. In limited areas, doctoral programs and the research needs of faculty and any post-masters graduate students at FAU-Broward and FIU-Broward will be served, to some extent by the collection in the University/College Library, and supplemented by ILL and the collections and services at the central campuses of FAU and FIU.

It is also important to understand that the consultant's study is only concerned with the Davie operation of both institutions. The "Agreement Between Florida Atlantic University and Broward Community College," dated 2/22/90, specifically refers to the facilities *and* services on the College Central Campus-Davie. No mention is made of the Broward County Public Library or the University Tower library services provided by FAU-Broward. It is recommended that the librarian responsible for the non-Davie Broward services also serve as a liaison between FAU-Broward and the library director of the UCL integrated library basically in the area of collection development (see Section on Staffing for more detail).

It is interesting to note that item 7 of the above mentioned agreement states that "preliminary discussions concerning the possibility of FAU entering into a contract with BCC to provide all personnel support required . . ." was considered as a possibility sometime in the future. My recommendations regarding staff certainly fall under that provision.

The problem of differing institution calendars requires that the academic library be open every day except for Easter, Thanksgiving, Christmas break and New Year's Day. The library would be closed for any legal holiday recognized by all three institutions. The library hours will be recommended by the library director and determined by the Governance/Policy Advisory Committee (GPAC). Staffing during Summer sessions, Spring breaks and holiday periods will be limited in level and number as determined by the library director. The staffing, however, must be adequate to assure an acceptable level of service to the library's clientele.

A chart showing the line of authority starting with the Presidents of FAU and BCC, followed by the Vice President-Broward and the Provost, BCC and finally the Governance/Policy Advisory Committee is included.

In the section on Governance, a shared governing/policy advisory committee, with administration and faculty members of BCC and FAU-Broward is recommended and described. FIU-Broward is represented by a non-voting academic faculty member. The make-up and responsibilities of the committee provide a balanced control of the library operation and make *certain* that the interests and academic requirements of *all three* institutions are fully and adequately met.

The section on the Academic Faculty Library Advisory Committee stresses the participation of faculty from the three institutions. The responsibility of the committee is with the library's overall service program. The committee serves as the advisory committee to the library director. Liaison relationship with the Governance/Policy Advisory Committee is recommended. A library organization chart, indicating briefly, the basic responsibilities of the various offices, departments and units under the administration of a library director is included. In the section on Long Range Planning, the development of a realistic five-year plan that will address the academic requirements for the institutions and their respective faculties, staff and students, is outlined. The section on Finances describes, in detail, the financial obligations of the participating institutions necessary to support a program that will adequately meet the academic requirements. A suggested budget for 1996-97 is included to give some perspective on the scope of the financial requirements for the current facility and program and the future facility and program. The estimates are based on the financial information provided by FAU-Broward and BCC. A suggested budget amount for 1995-96 is also included. The 1994-95 budget has already been determined and is at about the same level as the current year.

In the section on Staffing, the professional, paraprofessional (library technician) and clerical staff required to support the academic program is addressed. The current limited professional and paraprofessional staff is inadequate, even at present, if the library is to provide a quality level of effective service to students and faculty, let alone to do so with the planned expansion of facilities and services in 1997. A search for a new library director needs to begin immediately, certainly no later than August, 1994 to assure a starting date before January 1995. A suggested description for the position of Library Director is included.

In the section on Collection Development, careful consideration was given to the role of an academic faculty library advisory committee, representative of all three institutions. In addition, it addressed the need to merge the current three (one FAU Central, one BCC Libraries and one BCC Central) collection development policies. Strengthening of the current collection to meet the needs of university and college faculty and student academic programs is a priority that must be addressed as soon as possible. The participation of faculty from all three institutions, with the help and support of experienced professional library staff, is needed if the effort is to succeed. Members of the committee must consist of faculty with strong subject background and interests. A process for student participation in collection development must be devised as soon after the first meeting of the advisory committee as possible. Broadening and strengthening a library collection is a long term process. If started immediately the expanded and strengthened collection can meet the program needs of the universities and the community college currently as well as the expanded program when the move into the new facility is completed. More effective use of the current budget is essential to starting the process as soon as possible.

The area of Automated Systems and Computer Technologies is briefly addressed, focusing on basics and recognizing that the library director, the automated systems manager and the Associate Director for Public Services will need to review the current status, and based on the long range plan, make the necessary upgrading and expansion changes and additions.

A section on Evaluation of the organizational structural and operational agreement is included.

The last section of the report addresses the issue of Implementation. Based on acceptance of the study recommendation for an integrated University/College Library, it addresses the establishment of a Governance/Policy Advisory Committee, the recruiting of a library director, transition from current library status to an integrated library, establishing the academic faculty advisory committee, developing a new collection development policy and basic financing requirements. One additional item in the Implementation section is the suggestion for a temporary name: "University/College Library, and later, Learning Resources Center." The new facility will house both the library (UCL) and the learning resources center (LRC). There may be a need for a more distinctive name for the library; perhaps a donor who would like his/her name associated with the new facility can be found.

Reprinted with permission.

Common Ground:
Making Library Services Work
at a Collocated Campus

Cynthia Fugate

SUMMARY. This article describes the provision of library services to the collocated campuses of the University of Washington, Bothell and Cascadia Community College in Washington State. Important factors in success are: a good operating agreement, support and counsel of colleagues at other academic libraries, shared commitment to success, and frequent communication at all levels. *[Article copies available for a fee from The Haworth Document Delivery Service: 1-800-HAWORTH. E-mail address: <getinfo@haworthpress.com> Website: <http://www.HaworthPress.com> © 2001 by The Haworth Press, Inc. All rights reserved.]*

KEYWORDS. University of Washington, Bothell; Cascadia Community College; collocation; joint-use libraries; library cooperation

When speaking about partnerships, collaborations and other forms of cooperative endeavor, people are apt to say "Good fences make good neighbors," using this line from Robert Frost's poem "Mending Wall" to express the need for mutually agreed upon boundaries in any collective

Cynthia Fugate is Director, University of Washington, Bothell and Cascadia Community College Library in Bothell, WA.

Address correspondence to: Cynthia Fugate, Campus Library, Box 358550, 18225 Campus Way, NE, Bothell, WA 98011-8245 (E-mail: cfugate@bothell.washington.edu).

[Haworth co-indexing entry note]: "Common Ground: Making Library Services Work at a Collocated Campus." Fugate, Cynthia. Co-published simultaneously in *Resource Sharing & Information Networks* (The Haworth Information Press, an imprint of The Haworth Press, Inc.) Vol. 15, No. 1/2, 2001, pp. 55-64; and: *Joint-Use Libraries* (ed: William Miller, and Rita M. Pellen) The Haworth Information Press, an imprint of The Haworth Press, Inc., 2001, pp. 55-64. Single or multiple copies of this article are available for a fee from The Haworth Document Delivery Service [1-800-HAWORTH, 9:00 a.m. - 5:00 p.m. (EST). E-mail address: getinfo@haworthpress.com].

10.1300/J121v15n01_05

effort. While such boundaries are necessary, it is important also to focus on the narrator's remark, "Before I built a wall I'd ask to know/What I was walling in or walling out,/And to whom I was like to give offence" (Frost 1979, page 33-34). After the ink is dry on the boundary setting documents, so much in collaborative efforts depends on a willingness to trust one's partners' good intentions and on a commitment to succeed in spite of all the reasons to fail. At the University of Washington, Bothell and Cascadia Community College Library (Campus Library) we have been fortunate in our collaborators and partners, and have benefited from the extraordinary generosity of our colleagues at the University and at community colleges across the State. Throughout the process of building both institutions, we have relied on the counsel of many librarians and administrators (and on their resources as well) to create a library that can serve both institutions with passion and commitment.

HISTORY OF UWB/CCC COLLOCATION

In 1990, the University of Washington, Bothell opened its doors to students as one of five branch campuses in the State of Washington. The University of Washington, Tacoma is the other branch campus operated by the University of Washington; Washington State University has three branch campuses located in Spokane, the Tri-Cities, and Vancouver. All five branch campuses were charged by the Legislature and the state Higher Education Coordinating Board to serve the needs of time-bound, place-bound students. Although the University of Washington, Bothell is only 18 miles from the Seattle campus, highway gridlock and limits to growth at the Seattle campus contributed to the decision to establish a campus at Bothell.

The University of Washington, Bothell (UWB) provides upper division (junior and senior) and graduate education in a variety of disciplines. The campus started with a student body of 100 pioneers, and has grown in 12 years to over 1,200 full-time equivalent students. The campus currently offers a number of undergraduate programs, including Liberal Studies, Environmental Science, Nursing, Business, and Computing and Software Systems, as well as K-8 Teacher Certification. Graduate programs include Master's degrees in Business Administration, Education, Policy Studies and Nursing. UWB is an innovative, student-centered institution where collaboration between faculty and librarians is expected and supported.

The establishment of a three-campus university has not been an easy task for faculty and administrators. The original impulse to create two new semi-autonomous and fiscally independent entities has evolved to a somewhat more integrated approach that might be described as inter-dependent and complementary. Still, issues of faculty governance, campus autonomy, control of curriculum, and responsibility for strate-gic and capital planning continue to be raised. Despite this history, the University of Washington Libraries has always viewed the Bothell and Tacoma campus libraries as 2 of the more than 20 units that comprise the University of Washington Libraries. (Indeed, for the first ten years, there was a single Director overseeing both of the branch campuses and reporting to the Director of University Libraries. With the evolution of the campuses, there are now Directors at each campus, also reporting to the Director of University of Washington Libraries.) Being parts of the whole has many advantages for library staff as well as for students and faculty. Although appointments are local to UWB, librarians achieve permanent status (a tenure-like process) by satisfying system-wide cri-teria for advancement and are evaluated by peers throughout the Li-braries. Library staff, faculty and students enjoy the best of both worlds–access to a world-class library and its expertise, and a smaller scale that allows for experimentation and rapid change. Within the Uni-versity of Washington, the Libraries are often cited as the example of how three-campus cooperation ought to happen, and this foundation in collaboration served us well when the decision was made to collocate with a new community college.

In 1994, Washington State officials decided that the state's newest community college, Cascadia, and the University of Washington, Bothell should be joint occupants of what was then known as Truly Farm. UWB had been occupying rented quarters in a business park since its opening in 1990 and had already started the design process for its new campus.

On the other hand, Cascadia Community College was newly hatched, having been created to address the educational needs of a rapidly grow-ing population in the North King/South Snohomish County region. The standard arguments for collocation often stress the efficiencies to be gained in combining support and/or administrative functions, and the leveraging of resources made possible by sharing expensive operations. The collocation of UWB and Cascadia was certainly driven by those factors, but there was a space imperative as well. In this densely popu-lated corner of Puget Sound, there was very little buildable land left, and the decision to collocate was, in part, made because of the difficulty of locating appropriate building sites for two institutions. Like most solu-tions, though, it has a limited life span–the current site will accommodate up to 10,000 combined FTE. Should campus-wide growth exceed that number, as is expected, one of the institutions will need to relocate. It is, of course, possible that wider acceptance of distance learning or continued lack of state funding for higher education will make expansion unnecessary or impossible, but neither of those scenarios is the accepted wisdom at the moment.

As part of the establishing legislation, both Cascadia and UWB were instructed to share services wherever possible. Included in the list of shared services are physical plant, security, and some student services. It was inevitable that the library would emerge as a prime candidate for joint use. The appeal of shared library services to policymakers is obvious: one building to build and maintain, no duplication of staff, shared collections and services.

Usually when a decision to collocate is made, the libraries at the participating institutions must struggle to merge staff, services, and cultures. In this case, we were fortunate that our task involved not the merging of two existing systems but the grafting of a new twig onto an existing plant. At the time the collocation decision was made, Cascadia was still in the planning phase and had no students, and very few staff. Conversely, UWB had been in operation for ten years in its temporary quarters and had a fully staffed and functional library with a history of student and faculty-centered service. Thus, we believe, we were able to avoid many of the problems that arise when existing systems try to merge.

PLANNING FOR SUCCESS

At the top, the planning effort was led by dedicated administrators who believed in the importance of each party having a full understanding of what each institution could bring to the partnership, as well as an acknowledgment of where institutional missions might diverge. The Dean of the University of Washington, Bothell and the President of Cascadia Community College negotiated a set of operating principles, which informed the planning at all levels. These principles underlie all subagreements that are negotiated to operationalize the collocation. In the case of the library, a critical principle has been that neither institution will underwrite the operations of the other. In other words, shared library services should not result in either the University or the College paying more than its fair share for services or resources available to its students or faculty.

Planning shared library and media services and designing the new library building involved staff at all levels, from the University of Washington Libraries, the Campus Library and from community colleges in the region. We were lucky to be planning a new campus as well as a collocation. Since we were performing both tasks simultaneously, we were able to create spaces that encourage and support shared effort such as enough group study rooms, information literacy classrooms, and a multimedia development lab. Equally important, we were able to negotiate sufficient budgets to staff the new library adequately so there was no sense of added burden for the staff who had worked at the UWB temporary site.

We were particularly fortunate to have the advice of a number of community college librarians in planning our new library and its services. For accreditation purposes, Cascadia operated under the umbrella of Shoreline Community College, and several community college librarians from Shoreline and from other colleges in the region helped to launch the planning effort. There were many joint planning committees with faculty from UWB, Shoreline, and other colleges helping to plan the new buildings and to explore areas of collaboration in administrative and academic services. The Director of the Library Media Services at Shoreline Community College was appointed to chair the Library Media Technology Computing Subcommittee. Along with committee members from community colleges and the university, his subcommittee worked to describe ideal library services and facilities at the collocated campus. UWB librarians and UW Libraries administrators were involved in the planning efforts, staffing working groups which addressed the philosophy of the proposed library, and of the information literacy program, and providing final review of the report. This first opportunity to share our philosophies of service and pedagogy was heartening as we discovered many common values, a shared passion for excellence, and a mutual commitment to students as our first priority.

After the initial phase described above, focused facilities planning continued intensively from 1995-2000 when the new campus was finished. Community college faculty and staff throughout the region worked with UWB colleagues, planners, and architects to envision the physical structures that would give form to our sometimes shared, sometimes divergent vision. As part of the capital planning process, the project architect, NBBJ, organized a collocation workshop to which it invited administrators from a number of collocated institutions around the country. From the experiences shared at the workshop, it became clear that the dynamic tension we were experiencing between the desire for a separate institutional identity and the practical need to provide joint services was not only perfectly normal, but healthy. A joint venture composed of equal partners is interesting and exciting, but also complex and in constant need of tending. Several architectural features were devised to express the unique identities of the institutions: while the exterior of the buildings (brick) are the same, small details differ, such as the slight variations in color of the contrasting fascia on each building; each institution has a signature color that is used in the same prominent place in every building to reinforce the separate institutional identities; and finally, the furniture in each building, while thematically linked via a retro 1930s *art moderne* style, has distinctive colors and fabrics associated with each institution.

Since it was clear from the beginning that the Campus Library would be a shared service, we were able to focus on operations at an earlier stage than our colleagues planning other areas of the campus. At the administrative level, discussions began between the Director of the UW Bothell and Tacoma Libraries and Cascadia's Vice President for Student Learning exploring the limits and possibilities of shared library and media services. This process was iterative, with several drafts going out for review over the course of more than a year. It was decided that Cascadia would contract for library and media (including classroom support) services from the University Libraries, and that those services would be performed locally via the Campus Library staff, augmented by staff hired under the subagreement and financed by Cascadia. In the end, the details were spelled out in a Library and Media Services subagreement to the "Cascadia Community College and University of Washington, Bothell Operation and Management Foundation Agreement." The basic principle informing the subagreement is equity–attempting to provide equal services to Cascadia students in exchange for appropriate financial considerations. Services are provided to Cascadia on a proportional basis calculated on the number of full-time equivalent students, and the costs are recalculated as the institutions grow. Those services are provided by the entire library system, not by Campus Library staff alone. In fact, most technical services are provided by the University Libraries' Seattle campus, with some local processing performed at the Campus Library. Cascadia students, faculty and staff are entitled to access the full array of services and collections available to the University community on the same terms that UWB students, faculty and staff enjoy. These services include access to databases and full-text electronic resources through the Libraries Gateway, daily courier service for books and other printed materials, delivery of electronic documents to the desktop, and access to Cascade, a joint catalog of the six public baccalaureate institutions in Washington State.

During the deliberations it was decided that classroom support was one area where customization was possible. Cascadia was given a choice of three levels of support, a menu of tiered services with the midrange being equivalent to the level of support provided to UWB. In the end, although they could have chosen to pay for more or less support, they chose the midrange, and are provided with services identical to those offered to UWB.

In the Fall and Winter of 2000/01 the Director of the UW Bothell/ Cascadia Campus Library and the Vice President for Student Learning at Cascadia negotiated a biennial agreement for 01-03. In that document, the principles and practices remain the same, with minor changes to reflect lessons learned in the first year. For example, the original agreement required additional payment for course integrated library instruction that involved more than a couple of visits by a librarian to a class. After experimenting with this model for a year, the limitation was removed from the agreement at the request of the Libraries, since it was counter to the Libraries' mission to provide effective information literacy instruction. As we approach the negotiation of the 03-05 agreement both parties seem happy with the current model, although some adjustments are expected.

At the campus level, Campus Library and Media Center staff worked with colleagues from the community colleges to refine our understanding of how community colleges used their libraries and media centers, and what new or modified services we could look forward to offering. In addition, we consulted extensively with Debra Gilchrist, Director of Pierce College Library, about cost models for community college library services and about how to create an information literacy program for community college students. As an authority in the field, her advice was extraordinarily valuable and her endorsement of the staffing plan was key to its approval by the President of Cascadia. In Washington State, as elsewhere, the funding ratios for libraries in community colleges and university are radically different, with community colleges providing inexpensive education to a broad array of students. It was hard for administrators at Cascadia to understand why our staffing levels would be so much higher than those they were accustomed to in the community college system and they were surprised by our estimates of staffing needs. Cascadia ultimately contributed 10 staff, increasing existing staffing by almost a third.

Establishing the funding model was an important test of the primacy of the operating principles discussed above. An important principle declared that neither institution should underwrite the other, and an equally important corollary was that the quality of services offered to students should not suffer as a result of collocation. Putting these principles into practice meant that Cascadia was required to spend more of its budget on library and media services than other community colleges. In fact, in its first year of operation, the percentage of overall budget that Cascadia devoted to library and media services was twice the average expended by other community colleges in the state (State Board for Community and Technical Colleges, 2001, 87).

Working out the actual cost of providing library services on a per FTE basis was quite difficult, especially as we were afraid we might be comparing apples to oranges. We were hesitant to use existing cost data for the University Libraries because community college students use libraries differently and we wanted a model that reflected the actual conditions. On the other hand, we knew that Cascadia students would be exposed to a richer array of materials, and more importantly, perhaps, faculty would have more latitude in assignments knowing that students had access to the full suite of University of Washington resources and services. In the end, we extrapolated from the early UWB experience as a new and remote campus, and used that known data to develop staffing and cost models. Generally speaking, costs were distributed by FTE, so that Cascadia paid 40% of the cost and UWB paid 60% since that was the student FTE distribution when the first agreement was negotiated. There were some exceptions based on our anticipation of community college practice. Most notably, we agreed to bill on a per-item basis for some services we suspected would not be as popular with Cascadia students, such as document delivery. This prediction proved to be true, and Cascadia was billed for less than half of our original estimate of document delivery in the first year.

During the 01-02 academic year, Cascadia was preparing for its first accreditation visit. As part of that process, we surveyed students and staff about their satisfaction with library and media services, with very gratifying results: all measures were well over 90% positive. Cascadia has recently been granted candidacy status, and the Campus Library was particularly commended for the staff's pervasive and focused commitment to student and faculty success and for providing superior access to information resources.

COMMUNICATION–
KEEPING IN TOUCH WITH OUR PARTNERS

As part of the planning process, UWB librarians met in several workshop settings to discuss how we would meet the challenge of collocation. We decided that our mission was to create a library that serves community college and university students and faculty equally well. That means, among other things, making sure that the library is truly common ground–"owned" by the students and faculty of both institutions. As part of that process, it is important to make as many connections between the two institutions as possible. One tactic that has worked particularly well in creating bridges rather than boundaries is to assign to librarians similar liaison responsibilities across institutions, so that, for example, the Science Librarian serves the faculty and students of Cascadia and UWB. In the role of subject liaison, librarians select materials, provide specialized reference assistance, team-teach with faculty and serve on discipline-related committees. As librarians share what they know about curricula and programs, they have helped to connect faculty members at each institution with one another, and to demystify the university for community college students.

As librarians committed to the integration of information literacy instruction into curricula, our approach to working with both UWB and Cascadia has been to be as involved as possible in the life of the institutions. We have been fortunate to be present at the creation of two outstanding, innovative schools and have found that the best way to become part of a community is to help to create it. Operating on the theory that they won't complain about you if you're in the room, librarians have pursued opportunities to work at institution building. For example, librarians participated fully in the curriculum planning process at Cascadia. They were invited to planning sessions that took place in the summer prior to opening the campus and helped teaching faculty to integrate concepts of information literacy into the curriculum. Librarians also serve on the Learning Outcome Teams, which are the organizational units of the College, and on key committees that oversee curriculum and academic planning. There is a similar level of involvement at UWB, where librarian participation ranges from serving as affiliate faculty and teaching credit-bearing classes to service on a myriad of program and University level committees.

The Director of the Campus Library serves on cabinet-level bodies at both institutions and in the Libraries. The main benefit to be derived is keeping lines of communication open–hearing the concerns of each body about various aspects of collocation and representing the values and mission of one constituency to another is a challenging and educational experience. It also serves to demonstrate that building bridges between the two institutions has become a key contribution that library staff at all levels make–from the Information Commons desk to the Boardroom, the mission is the same.

COOPERATION–A CONTINUING COMMITMENT

There are many examples of inter-institutional cooperation–stewardship of the campus wetlands, career counseling, transfer pathways for students, and jointly sponsored cultural events to name a few. The Campus Library does its share, as well, and in a recent move to get the faculty of both institutions better connected, we offered to provide space for each institution's teaching learning center–provided they would share the workroom and seminar room. We believe this proximity has helped to foster communication and will lead to meaningful collaboration. We hope that the students will benefit from the anticipated collaboration as well. Working through these centers librarians hope to be able to build an information literacy curriculum for our community college students that will articulate effectively with the curriculum already in place at UWB, thus establishing intellectual common ground as well.

Our plan is to insure that the Campus Library continues to be not only a virtual intellectual commons for our two communities, but an actual one as well. By welcoming students and faculty of both institutions and providing equal yet appropriately customized services and materials, we have tried to make the Campus Library a jointly held and valued resource. We have built our collocation on the cooperative efforts of legislators, administrators, librarians, faculty and staff–all of whom were willing to take a risk to provide access to high quality educational opportunities for the people of our region. It is gratifying to be able to report that collocation is going very well at UWB/CCC–thanks to a good foundation agreement, realistic cost models, frequent communication, and staff involvement at all levels of both institutions.

REFERENCES

Frost, Robert. 1979. *The Poetry of Robert Frost*. Edited by Edward Connery Lathem. New York: Henry Holt.
State Board for Community and Technical Colleges. 2001. *Academic Year Report*. Olympia, WA: State Board for Community and Technical Colleges. [cited July 15, 2001]. Available from the World Wide Web: <http://www.sbctc.ctc.edu/oldweb/Pub/PubAYR.htm>.

A Joint University, College and Public Library

Patricia Roshaven
Rudy Widman

SUMMARY. Florida Atlantic University, Indian River Community College, and the St. Lucie County Library developed a joint-use library facility serving the information needs of three distinct populations. This article reviews planning, staffing, managing, and collection development issues encountered by the partners of the joint-use library. The complex nature of the operation is described through interviews with library staff and library administrators. Agreements between the cooperating libraries are included. *[Article copies available for a fee from The Haworth Document Delivery Service: 1-800-HAWORTH. E-mail address: <getinfo@haworthpress.com> Website: <http://www.HaworthPress.com> © 2001 by The Haworth Press, Inc. All rights reserved.]*

KEYWORDS. Joint-use library, joint venture, self-managed teams, joint-use agreements, library cooperation, Florida Atlantic University, Indian River Community College, St. Lucie County Library

Patricia Roshaven, MLS, is Associate University Librarian, Florida Atlantic University, 5353 Parkside Drive, Jupiter, FL 33458 (E-mail: roshaven@fau.edu).

Rudy Widman, PhD, is Assistant Dean of Learning Resources, Indian River Community College, 3209 Virginia Avenue, Ft. Pierce, FL 34981 (E-mail: rwidman@ircc.cc.fl.us).

The authors would like to thank Dr. Susan Taggart, Susan Kilmer, Carla Robinson, Hazal Taatjes, Mary Beth Pickney, Wanda Johnson, Leslie Hoyt, and Linda Lesperance for their permission to be interviewed for this article.

[Haworth co-indexing entry note]: "A Joint University, College and Public Library." Roshaven, Patricia, and Rudy Widman. Co-published simultaneously in *Resource Sharing & Information Networks* (The Haworth Information Press, an imprint of The Haworth Press, Inc.) Vol. 15, No. 1/2, 2001, pp. 65-87; and: *Joint-Use Libraries* (ed: William Miller, and Rita M. Pellen) The Haworth Information Press, an imprint of The Haworth Press, Inc., 2001, pp. 65-87. Single or multiple copies of this article are available for a fee from The Haworth Document Delivery Service [1-800-HAWORTH, 9:00 a.m. - 5:00 p.m. (EST). E-mail address: getinfo@haworthpress.com].

10.1300/J121v15n01_06

INTRODUCTION

There are many joint-use libraries today that serve two population groups. In most cases users include college students and university students, people from the community and elementary or middle school students, or other combinations of two different groups. This article is about a joint-use facility involving three population groups: community college students, university students, and people from the community. The history of the project and current contractual agreements that make it possible are discussed along with insights from the library staff.

Florida Atlantic University, Indian River Community College, and the St. Lucie County Library System have been sharing a library facility since 1995, with a small staff that serves both the general public and the two academic communities on a small joint-use campus, in a newly developing community between Orlando and West Palm Beach, Florida. How did this arrangement come about, and how does it currently work?

BEGINNING OF THE PARTNERSHIP

The idea of a joint-use library began in 1988 when IRCC and Barry University both built branch campuses in the newly developed St. Lucie West area. Indian River Community College received funding to build a 10,000 square foot library at the IRCC St. Lucie West Campus in 1991 and signed a letter of intent to pursue a joint-use library with St. Lucie County. During the next several years Florida Atlantic University, one of the state universities in Florida, purchased the Barry University Building adjacent to the IRCC branch campus. IRCC, FAU, and St. Lucie County each needed a library to serve the needs of its users. The idea of a three-way joint-use venture appeared to be the most effective way to use limited resources to accomplish this objective.

After several years of negotiating, the library opened its doors in 1995. IRCC provided the building, utilities, and maintenance, and contracted with FAU to staff the library and furnish books and equipment. One staff member was an FAU employee and the others were IRCC employees paid with funds provided by FAU. Simultaneously, IRCC entered into a separate agreement with the St. Lucie County Library System to serve the general public in exchange for one staff member, operating expenses, staff, and a book collection geared to the public's needs.

State funding was obtained several years later to build an Indian River Community College/Florida Atlantic University joint-use campus to provide seamless four year baccalaureate degree programs, the first and second year offered by IRCC and the third and fourth year by FAU. A 15,000 square foot joint-use library was part of this expanded campus, along with several other buildings, and in January 2002 all three partners opened the library doors to provide seamless library services for university and college students as well as public library users.

In this case, ownership and maintenance of the facility are equally shared by IRCC and FAU. FAU provides three staff and the collection that supports upper division and graduate students. IRCC provides the collection for the first two years of study and a 20-hour per week paraprofessional. Library services for the public are provided through a contractual arrangement between IRCC and the St. Lucie County Public Library System, which provides three additional staff, and the public-library-oriented part of the book collection. All staff, with the exception of the FAU librarians, are supervised by IRCC. The FAU librarians are supervised by FAU.

STAFFING

One critical factor for the success of this joint-use venture is the joint-use library staff. They are in one of the most demanding roles in the profession as they must deal with three distinct library philosophies and translate them into unified values of the joint-use library. The staff is infused with a pioneering spirit requiring them to communicate effectively, advocate their positions, and negotiate to reach their goal. They work as a self-managed team in a culture of cooperation and commitment to ensure the successful operation of the library.

So far, it has not been necessary to prioritize service. Staff has always been able to serve those who are waiting at the Desk; Library Instruction sessions are scheduled in advance so that staff is available when needed. An FAU librarian will instruct the FAU students, but if an FAU librarian is not available, County staff are willing and able to step in.

MANAGING

Managing this joint-use library involves considerable communication regarding separate policy development and planning, and negotiations and deliberations over issues with the other stakeholders. Monthly meetings are held with staff and partner institution administrations, and frequent management meetings are held throughout the year. Every year the agreements for services are evaluated and renegotiated to ensure the interests of all groups are represented and to support the work of the staff through budget priorities. The management team tries to ensure that "turf wars" are kept out of the management of the library. A primary reason this cooperative venture is able to flourish is the administrative commitment of all three governing bodies to provide an integrated library operated to the mutual benefit of all parties and their customers.

LIBRARY RESOURCES

St. Lucie County contributes to the book collection by providing general interest books through a rental agreement with Baker and Taylor and reference material through direct purchase. Access to all St. Lucie County branch library holdings is available to users. Some traditional public library functions like children's programs, young adult programs, and certain specialized collections are not supported at this library. IRCC and FAU also supply circulating and reference books that support the curriculum of each entity. The combined book collection is over 26,000 volumes and is expected to double within five years. The Library of Congress classification system is used to catalog library items for all three institutions.

ELECTRONIC RESOURCES

Electronic information resources from each partner are also made available to library users. Three separate online catalogs and networks are installed in the library: a DRA system for the community college, a NOTIS system for the university catalog, and SIRSI for the public library catalog. Partners also provide access to their home library electronic databases through dedicated networks. Library management functions, like circulation, for IRCC and FAU are handled through the College Center for Library Automation DRA system while public library transactions are handled through their SIRSI system. Eventually, the community college and university will move to a joint online system, along with the other community colleges and state universities in Florida.

Patrons may not be aware that there are separate catalogs and checkout systems. The online catalogs of all three institutions are available on all computers, but IRCC students are trained to use IRCC databases, FAU students learn how to use FAU databases and County residents are shown how to use the County catalog. FAU's and IRCC's check-out systems are combined, and the County check-out computer is adjacent, which makes it easy to provide seamless service.

PERSPECTIVE OF ST. LUCIE WEST LIBRARY STAFF

To get a first-hand perspective on the challenges and opportunities of working in a three-way library, we interviewed the staff, and occasionally quoted from articles on joint ventures and self-managed teams to prompt their thinking. Staff comments are a reflection of their experiences at the St. Lucie West Library and on the articles listed in the selected bibliography, below. Those who were interviewed have been part of this self-managed team for the past five or six years. Dr. Susan Taggart, Provost of the IRCC/FAU St. Lucie West Campus, and Susan Kilmer, Director of the St. Lucie County Library System, were also interviewed.

Dr. Taggart advocates for all members of the community: public library users, community college and university. She said, *"Now that technology is so much a part of everyone's life, I would like to see all members of the community receive training in library technology and library databases. The marriage of these three organizations is wonderful. The staff is willing to help everyone. I have heard only positive comments about the library."*

Susan Kilmer underscored the problems of a joint-use facility when she said that discussions were held between IRCC and the St. Lucie County Library System before she became Director in 1988, but the two institutions were not able to come to an agreement about which collection and which catalog would be dominant. It was after the IRCC Library was built at St. Lucie West and the idea was again discussed, that agreement was made. The County definitely wants to remain in this joint venture. *"It has worked very well for the public side. It is very seldom that you have the opportunity to have these resources for the public in a branch facility at such low operating costs. If we see more and more younger families living in St. Lucie West, we may need to create a children's collection and the library may need to adjust to having children and teen programs."*

When the staff were asked how they keep their allegiances straight, they said that they are loyal to the St. Lucie West Library, not to whom they report or the institution that signs their paychecks.

Person A: *We tend to put aside our own self-interests. The name of the game here is compromise for the good of the team. Our main goal is to keep our patrons happy. We assess the needs of each individual and then give them the assistance they need.*

Interviewer: *It must be tough to compromise so often.*

Person A: *Yes, many compromises come because FAU policies are this and IRCC policies are that and the County's policies are something else. We are constantly challenged. An example is rules about children in the library. The County library allows children in the library over the age of 12 without a parent or guardian, the community college and university libraries require that they be 18. Of course, if a 16 year old is taking classes at IRCC or FAU, that student is allowed in the library without a parent. We find that we have to blur the rules between the three different systems. Service to our patrons is our primary goal. A joint-use minimum age policy is under discussion at this time.*

Person B: *I can't tell you the number of times we've gone into meetings and had differences of opinion but we have all come out of that meeting smiling, ready to go back to work with each other. Sometimes we are competitive with each other, but that keeps us alive and on our toes.*

JOINT VENTURE CONTRACT

Joint ventures have differing policies, procedures and cultures, yet must create an organization in which their benefits are maximized. If this melding of organizations fails, the joint venture fails. Contracts are written which bind the parties together in a legal sense. It is up to the employees to ensure that the contracts work.

Interviewer: *According to Woodside et al. (1996, 26), "Even though the joint venture has a contractual structure, the problem of moral hazard still arises. The contract is insufficient for two reasons (Arrow 1985). First, it is impossible to specify all contingencies. Second, even if it were possible to cover all contingencies, it would be impossible to enforce such a contract. This reality implies that other means beyond the contract must be found to monitor and control the principal-agent relationship."*

Person C: *That's us! We are the people keeping the contract.*

Interviewer: *"Moral hazards" cause tensions in the workplace and undermine the viability of the joint venture. For example, one party may hide information from the other, or insist on certain procedures without gaining the cooperation of the other parties. "In order for the joint venture to succeed, each partner must relinquish some autonomy to the other" (Woodside et al. 1996, 25).*

Person D: *Relinquishing autonomy–this is what it comes down to, isn't it?*

THE SELF-MANAGED TEAM

An excellent antidote to these potential difficulties is the self-managed team. If the members of the team are carefully chosen, they will be unusual people: they will value group decisions, assume responsibility for themselves within the team and for the success of the team, have a strong work ethic, be goal-oriented, proactive, conscientious, tend to be extraverted, agreeable, soft-hearted and open to experience (Kirkman et al. 2001; Thoms et al. 2002). [NOTE: Information from Kirkman, Thoms, and Maddi comes from numerous pages in these articles.] Maddi et al. 1991 adds that hardy team members have strong coping skills, are intelligent, credible and creative. According to Maddi (121), their "research indicates that only about one third of working adults are reasonably hardy."

Team members with the above traits will be committed to success, be natural problem solvers, will thrive on open communication and will be able to minimize the inherent difficulties of a joint venture. In a manager-led organization, employees are responsible only to the manager and not to each other, making it possible to hide actions and information. The successful self-managed team requires openness from everyone on the team.

Person B: *The last six years have been an eye-opener in human nature and how different people react to each other. It's always a learning situation. Because this is a self-managed team, everything happens in the open, so you can see everyone for what they are.*

Person D: *We are willing to negotiate, to talk things out and come to a consensus. People are willing to give up some of their views for the collective good of the library. This makes an enormous difference. I don't think we have a lot of ego in this group. It's the large ego that needs to hide. It is really important to be able to express your feelings honestly without retaliation. No one bears a grudge. When we walk out of a meeting, we are still friends.*

Person E: *If we work hard, we can be successful. Difficulties tend to make our team stronger.*

Although self-managed work teams are reputed to increase productivity and employee commitment, "only 10% of workers are in SMWTs in the organizations that use them" (Thoms et al. 2002, 27). Not everyone is willing or able to adapt in order to be successful in a self-managed work team.

Interviewer: *"Instead of having a supervisor tell them what to do, members regulate their own behavior, gather and synthesize information, make important decisions, and take collective responsibility for meeting team goals"* (Thoms et al. 2002, 4).

Person A: *If you prefer managers to tell you what to do, you would not be comfortable in self-managed teams. It is comforting to have someone else think through problems. It would be very hard for me to go back to a system with a boss who makes all the decisions and did not listen to what I have to say.*

Person E: *As a group, we are the authority.*

Interviewer: *You have all been together for a long time. Was it difficult when you were all figuring out what it meant to be "self-managed"?*

Person F: *It was difficult in the sense that I did not understand it, but it was not difficult because everyone is so open. We are all willing to help each other. To this day, one of our favorite lines is, "I am still learning." What is the policy and procedure today might change. The important thing is that everyone shares information. It takes time to know the policies and resources of all the institutions.*

Interviewer: *You have people on your staff with strong opinions.*

Person A: *We are all strong women; we are not afraid to say what we are thinking. If we see trouble with what someone is doing, we have a frank discussion with this person, inside or outside the staff meetings. No one is afraid to speak her mind.*

Person F: *We thrive on sparks. If someone didn't rattle the cage we would wonder what was going on. Sometimes if we have part-time or new people, we are on them all the time because we don't want them saying things that are not true. Our credibility is on the line. We step in and say something immediately. The bottom line is that we want people to say, "This is a good staff."*

Person E: *We are strongly motivated to learn more about our jobs and to set our goals to a higher level.*

Person C: *Occasionally someone will get discouraged with the difficulties that we have to resolve, but it passes. Everyone needs to be articulate, and to be willing to stand fire from other members of the team. You have to be able to put your ego aside. As in any relationship, we go along smoothly for awhile, and then through an adjustment. But as a whole team, I think we work well. We can always turn to a supervisor when we get stuck.*

Interviewer: *Not all employees are willing to take on the autonomy and responsibility that are required in a self-managed team.*

Person A: *We are all concerned when there is a new hire because that person has to fit in. From day one we were told that regardless of our degree, our input would be valued and that was one of the main things that attracted me when I began as a work-study at the IRCC Library. When the St. Lucie West Library was formed, the whole idea was to get people here who believed in that.*

Person F: *Everybody, in essence, was handpicked. The blend is so important.*

Person D: *Yes! We all see ourselves as leaders and committed to the same goals. We have similar views on the broad issues. When we have to talk out differences, it usually helps to take a broad perspective. An example was the phone message system, which one person wanted and everyone else did not. We were able to keep part of the message system, such as leaving our hours available for patrons to listen to, but patrons are not able to renew a book on the phone because not all books, such as Interlibrary Loans, can be renewed. This decision involved a lot of negotiation, but it was resolved to everyone's satisfaction.*

Interviewer: *What is your greatest challenge?*

Person B: *Keeping lines of communication open. We have to be sure that everyone knows what they need to know. That is, if there is a change at FAU that affects everyone, we have to share this information. When the FAU bookstore opened, I told the rest of the staff because students will be asking us where the bookstore is and when it is open. Another example is the use of the library display case, which was purchased with FAU money. There is some pressure to have only academic displays. We will need to have a meeting about this.*

Person D: *Staying abreast of all the changing information while providing the best possible service is, I think, the greatest challenge. There are the policies and resources of three institutions to be aware of and three sets of library users, each with different needs.*

Person F: *Maintaining a sense of balance within the realm of hourly, daily, monthly and yearly change. Because adapting to change and problem solving are constants at this joint-use library, a balanced outlook, or returning to a balanced state, is essential. To some, an issue is like a small pebble gently being tossed into a pond. The result is a little ripple in the water. To others, the same issue is like a huge boulder crashing into the pond. The result is a tsunami. Striving for balance requires sensitivity, listening, patience, and time.*

Person A: *Our biggest challenge is forces outside our control. All three of the institutions have their own policies and systems. That FAU allowed the IRCC computer system to be dominant was a big concession and involved considerable negotiation. Every day is an adventure here!*

Each person closed the interview with a similar statement, here in Person C's words: *"I like working here. I like the joint-use facility. We have our problems. We have personalities we have to put up with, we have situations that arise that make us very uncomfortable, and then we have to work to get back to homeostasis. I would say that our team is made up of intelligent, creative, thoughtful people. I feel blessed to be part of this. For everything we have been through as a team, I think the value to the community is immeasurable. We offer resources that as one institution we couldn't possibly offer. I feel very proud to be part of it.*"

Clearly, staff responses show that harmony has been maintained through a union of head and heart. There have been many times when they have re-forged their alliance in the cauldron of staff meetings. St. Lucie West staff exhibit a characteristic not mentioned so far: an old-fashioned belief that the struggle inherent in a long-term commitment has benefited them personally as well as professionally.

MUTUAL BENEFITS

So, what are the benefits of a three party joint-use library? The fundamental benefit is that without the IRCC, FAU, and St. Lucie County cooperation no library would be available to the library users of each entity, at least not a library with access to the vast resources currently available with limited funding. The joint-use library provides an integrated approach to both academic communities using the joint-use campus and to the local residents. It provides resources not normally available at a single entity library including access to more staff, extended opening hours, flexibility in providing and obtaining resources, access to information on university, college, and community services, and an opportunity to promote the services of each partner.

CHALLENGES AND OPPORTUNITIES

Joint-use libraries are an anomaly in traditional organizations and require constant attention. Often staff loses familiarity with resources of the "mother" institutions, necessitating frequent briefing meetings about available resources. Considerable time and effort are allocated to ensure that staff is knowledgeable about changing resources and services through in-service training.

Another challenge is to provide hours of operation to the satisfaction of all three partners. The end result is that this library is open to accommodate the needs of each individual entity. One future opportunity includes strengthening the team management approach to accommodate library users' needs and the needs of each partner and to increase the commitment to provide resources and services. A challenge is to make the apportionment of institutional expenditures more equal to the benefits each institution receives.

CONCLUSIONS

The St. Lucie West Library has met the challenge of establishing and providing a three-way joint-use operation by creating a dynamic information resource. The goal of providing a service equal to or better than that provided by the separate entities was met but continues to evolve. The joint-use library is popular, exciting, and a manifestation of community vision and professional commitment. The key factor that makes the St. Lucie West Library a good joint-use library is the library staff who rise to their challenges and opportunities. We see no definitive end point to reach but a continuing search to achieve the ultimate information resource for our students and the community. The ongoing challenge will be to maintain harmony between groups with conflicting needs.

SELECTED BIBLIOGRAPHY

Arrow, Kenneth J. 1985. "The Economics of Agency." In *Principals and Agents: The Structure of Business,* edited by J.W. Pratt and R.J. Zeckhauser. Boston: Harvard Business School Press.

Kirkman, Bradley L. and Shapiro, Debra L. "The Impact of Team Members' Cultural Values on Productivity, Cooperation, and Empowerment in Self-Managing Work Teams." *Journal of Cross-Cultural Psychology* 32 (2001): 597-617.

Maddi, Salvatore R., Khoshaba, Deborah M. and Pammenter, Arthur. "The Hardy Organizations: Success by Turning Change to Advantage." *Consulting Psychology Journal: Practice and Research* 51 (1999): 117-124.

Thoms, Peg, Pinto, Jeffrey K., Parente, Diane R. and Druskat, Vanessa Urich. "Adaptation to Self-Managing Work Teams." *Small Group Research* 33 (2002): 1, 3-31.

Woodside, Arch G. and Pitts, Robert E., eds. *Creating and Managing International Joint Ventures.* Westport: Quorum Books, 1996.

APPENDIX I

AGREEMENT
Between
INDIAN RIVER COMMUNITY COLLEGE
and
FLORIDA ATLANTIC UNIVERSITY
Relating to
THE PROVISION OF LIBRARY SERVICES AT ST. LUCIE WEST

This is an Agreement made by and between the DISTRICT BOARD OF TRUSTEES of INDIAN RIVER COMMUNITY COLLEGE, a political subdivision of the State of Florida, ("IRCC") and the FLORIDA ATLANTIC UNIVERSITY, acting for and on behalf of the Florida Atlantic University Board of Trustees, ("FAU") to provide a joint use library at the St. Lucie West Campus.

The parties to this Agreement have determined that it would be to the mutual advantage of each and in the best interest of the faculty, staff, and students of Indian River Community College and Florida Atlantic University and to the citizens of St. Lucie County to provide for the joint use of library facilities.

In consideration of the mutual advantages accruing to the parties and the benefits, promises, and considerations hereinafter set out, IRCC and FAU agree as follows:

I. PURPOSE AND INTENT

IRCC and FAU wish to maximize the use of their respective resources and to provide state-of-the-art information services for the students and faculty of Indian River Community College and Florida Atlantic University, and the residents of St. Lucie County. It is further the intent of the parties:

A. To provide high quality library services to faculty and students of IRCC and FAU and to the public at large.
B. To ensure that library standards, as specified by the Southern Association of Colleges and Schools, are met.
C. To maximize the use of funds and facilities for libraries to avoid unnecessary duplication of facilities and services.
D. To jointly provide programs and facilities that are better than either of the entities could provide on their own.
E. To further the relationship between IRCC, FAU, and the community.
F. To provide students and faculty of IRCC and FAU with access to the larger holdings of the Library.

II. ROLE OF THE PARTIES

In consideration of mutual covenants and promises herein contained, IRCC and FAU agree as follows:

A. Library services shall be provided to FAU and IRCC students and faculty and to the residents of St. Lucie County at the IRCC/FAU St. Lucie West Campus, as described below:

1. The responsibility for the administration of the library operations rests with the IRCC Head of Library Services and the FAU Director of Libraries.
2. The responsibility for the administration of the physical plant rests with the IRCC St. Lucie West Campus Provost and the FAU Treasure Coast Campus Vice President.
3. Library services shall include the use of IRCC, FAU, and St. Lucie County furnishings and equipment as determined jointly by all parties.
4. IRCC and FAU agree to provide funds for the operation of the library.
5. Of the operating budget for FY 2002/2003, of $_____$, FAU agrees to provide $\_\_\_\_\_$, IRCC agrees to provide $\_\_\_\_$ with the balance (exclusive of salaries, wages and benefits) of $_____$ provided by St. Lucie County. FAU and St. Lucie County will pay salaries, benefits and wages for authorized positions using the fiscal agency of IRCC.
6. For future fiscal years, the parties agree to meet on or before February 1 of each year beginning February 1, 2003, or when budget figures are available, to confer and develop a proposed operating budget.
7. FAU and IRCC will each directly purchase, disburse funds and account for their share of the operating budget; IRCC will act as the fiscal agent for disbursement of St. Lucie County Funds.
8. General library services and hours of operation shall be determined by mutual agreement between all parties and shall specifically provide the following:

   a. Processing, shelving, and maintenance of all books, periodicals, and other resources forwarded to the St. Lucie West site from the FAU Main Campus Library or the IRCC Main Campus Library or received directly at the site as a result of subscriptions or standing orders for print or non-print material.
   b. Reserve book operation, including the production and maintenance of a reserve book list.

   c. Reference assistance.
   d. Interlibrary loan services to FAU students and faculty, IRCC students and faculty and public patrons with the provision that the first access points are the respective libraries through courier or DLLI.
   e. Circulation of library materials without numerical limitation, including granting of semester borrowing privileges to FAU and IRCC faculty and, upon recommendation of a major advisor, to graduate students.
   f. Bibliographic orientation for individuals and for classes.
   g. FAU equipment and software will be maintained by FAU technicians, IRCC equipment and software by IRCC technicians.
   h. Using the services of the College Center for Library Automation (CCLA), IRCC will make available the LINCC online system at the St. Lucie West Library for library management purposes.
   i. FAU will provide LUIS for access to its bibliographic records and external databases.

9. IRCC shall contract with the St. Lucie County Library System to provide library resources for the citizens of St. Lucie County at the St. Lucie West Library.

III. FINANCIAL ARRANGEMENTS

A. IRCC shall provide current and cumulative financial data to FAU. IRCC shall also submit a monthly expense report for all expenditures of funds and shall provide year-end detailed reports. Such financial data and monthly or annual reports shall be sent to:

   1. Vice President, Treasure Coast Campus, Florida Atlantic University, 500 N.W. University Blvd., Port St. Lucie, FL 34986
   2. Associate Provost, Academic Affairs, Florida Atlantic University, 777 Glades Road, Boca Raton, FL 33431
   3. Director of University Libraries, Florida Atlantic University, 777 Glades Road, PO Box 3092, Boca Raton, FL 33431-0992

IRCC shall also furnish the above-named individuals copies of annual financial reports covering the Agreement year when distributed.

B. In the event of discontinuance of funding by the Florida Legislature in subsequent years, or the termination of this Agreement, all materials, furniture and equipment which have been purchased with FAU funds shall revert to FAU unless otherwise provided for in a subsequent agreement.

C. The total amount payable by FAU is agreed upon annually between IRCC and FAU. The budget for 2002-2003 is specified in the appendix to this Agreement.

D. Pursuant to Section 215.422(3)(b), Florida Statutes, a state agency shall mail IRCC's payment within forty (40) days after receipt of an acceptable invoice and receipt, and after inspection of the goods, services, or both, if provided in accordance with the terms and conditions of applicable purchase order/agreement. Failure to mail the warrant within 40 days shall result in the agency paying interest at the rate of one percent per month on the unpaid balance. The interest penalty shall be mailed within 15 days after mailing the warrant. A "Vendor Ombudsman" has been established with the Florida Department of Banking and Finance. The duties of this individual include acting as an advocate for vendors who may be experiencing problems in obtaining timely payments from a state agency. The Vendor Ombudsman may be contacted at (850) 488-2924, or by calling the State Comptroller's Hotline, 1-800-848-3792.

1. Partial payment in the full amount of the value of service received and accepted may be requested by the submission of a properly executed invoice, with supporting documents, if required.

2. IRCC agrees that bills and invoices for fees or other compensation for services or expenses shall cite the Agreement number and shall be submitted to the Controller in detail sufficient for a proper preaudit and postaudit of them. Each invoice must clearly identify the period of time for which compensation is sought. Payment will be rendered only for services or the portion of services completed prior to the submission of the invoice.

3. The performance of FAU of any of its obligations under this Agreement shall be subject to and contingent upon the availability of funds appropriated by the Legislature of the State of Florida, the obligation of funds by the prime funding agency, or otherwise lawfully expendable for the purposes of this Agreement for the current and future periods. FAU shall give notice to IRCC of the non-availability of such funds when FAU has knowledge of such fact. Upon receipt of such notice by IRCC, IRCC shall be entitled to payment only for those services performed and expenses incurred prior to the date notice is received.

E. Each party assumes any and all risk of personal injury, death and property damage attributable to the negligent acts or omissions of that party and its offices, employees and agents. IRCC also assumes such risk with respect to the negligent acts or of persons subcontracting with IRCC or otherwise acting or engaged to act at the instance of IRCC in furtherance of IRCC fulfilling IRCC's obligations under this Agreement.

F. IRCC shall allow public access to all documents, papers, letters or other material subject to the provisions of Chapter 119, Florida Statutes, and made or received by IRCC in conjunction with this Agreement. Refusal by IRCC to allow such public access shall be grounds for cancellation of this Agreement by FAU.

IV. TERM; TERMINATION

This Agreement shall be effective for a period of twenty (20) years beginning July 1, 2002; provided, however, that this Agreement shall be subject to cancellation by FAU or IRCC upon 90 days' written notice to either party. A cancellation penalty may not be charged to FAU or IRCC. FAU or IRCC shall be liable only for payment for services rendered, allowable expenses incurred, or both, prior to the effective date of termination within the limits of the description provided in Section I of this Agreement.

A. Any renewals, amendments, alterations, or modifications to the Agreement must be signed or initialed and approved by the signatories to this Agreement.

B. The validity, construction and effect of this Agreement shall be governed by the laws of the State of Florida. FAU and IRCC, as agencies of the State of Florida, are entitled to the benefits of sovereign immunity, including immunities from taxation. In the event either party is required to obtain from any governmental authority any permit, license, or authorization as a prerequisite to perform its obligations under this Agreement, the cost shall be borne by the party required to obtain such permit, license or authorization.

C. In accordance with Section 112.3185, Florida Statutes, IRCC certifies that to the best of its knowledge and belief, no individual employed by it or subcontracted by it has an immediate relation to any employee of FAU who was directly or indirectly involved in the procurement of the services described in this Agreement. Violation of this section by IRCC shall be grounds for cancellation of this Agreement by FAU.

D. IRCC may not, without the advance written approval of FAU, assign any right or delegate any duties under this Agreement, nor may it transfer, pledge, surrender or otherwise encumber or dispose of its interest in any portion of this Agreement.

E. Each term and condition of this Agreement is material, and any breach or default by IRCC in performance of each such term and condition shall be a material breach or default of the entire Agreement for which FAU shall have the right to terminate this Agreement immediately upon notice to IRCC and without termination penalty to FAU.

F. It is understood and agreed that nothing contained in this Agreement is intended, or should be construed, as creating or establishing the relationship of partners between the parties, or as constituting IRCC as the agent or representative of FAU for any purpose in any manner whatsoever. IRCC is not authorized to bind FAU to any contracts or other obligations. IRCC shall not expressly or impliedly represent to any party that IRCC and FAU are partners or that IRCC is the agent or representative of FAU or of the Board of Trustees of Florida Atlantic University for any purpose or in any manner whatsoever.

G. FAU's representative for purposes of this Agreement shall be the Vice President for the Treasure Coast Campus or his or her designee. IRCC's representative for purposes of this Agreement shall be the Provost of St. Lucie West Campus.

H. No failure to exercise or delay in exercising any right, power, or remedy accruing to FAU for any breach or default of IRCC under this Agreement shall impair any such right, power, or remedy of FAU or be construed as a waiver by FAU of any such breach or default or of any similar breach or default thereafter occurring; nor shall any waiver of any single breach or default be construed as a waiver of any other breach or default thereafter occurring.

I. All documents submitted are incorporated into this Agreement by reference. In the event of inconsistency between provisions, provisions of this Agreement will govern. This Agreement and such documents embody the entire agreement of both parties and there are no other representations, promises, agreements, conditions or understandings, either oral or written, between FAU and IRCC other than are set forth in this Agreement. No subsequent alteration, amendment, change or addition to this Agreement shall be binding upon either FAU or IRCC unless reduced to writing and signed by them and by direct reference made a part of this Agreement.

J. This Agreement is subject to the provisions of paragraph (2)(a) of Section 287.133, Florida Statutes, regarding public entity crimes.

IN WITNESS OF THE FOREGOING, the parties have signed this Agreement.

APPENDIX II

AGREEMENT
between
INDIAN RIVER COMMUNITY COLLEGE and ST. LUCIE COUNTY
relating to
THE PROVISION OF LIBRARY SERVICES AT ST. LUCIE WEST

This Interlocal Agreement is made by and between the DISTRICT BOARD OF TRUSTEES of INDIAN RIVER COMMUNITY COLLEGE, (hereinafter referred to as "Trustees") and ST. LUCIE COUNTY, a political subdivision of the State of Florida (hereinafter referred to as "County") to provide a joint use library.

WHEREAS, Trustees own real property including a 10,000 square foot library building at the St. Lucie West Campus; and,

WHEREAS, it is Trustee's desire to provide full library facilities for its students and faculty at the St. Lucie West Campus; and,

WHEREAS, it is County's desire to provide branch library services in the St. Lucie West area as part of the St. Lucie County Public Library System; and,

WHEREAS, the parties hereto have determined that it would be to the mutual advantage of each and in the best interest of both the citizens of St. Lucie County and the faculty, staff, and students of Indian River Community College to provide for the joint use of library facilities.

NOW, THEREFORE, in consideration of the mutual advantages accruing to the parties and the benefits, promises, and considerations hereinafter set out, Trustees and County agree as follows:

I. PURPOSE AND INTENT

Trustees and County wish to maximize the use of their respective resources and to provide state-of-the-art information services for the students and faculty of Indian River Community College and the residents of St. Lucie County. It is further the intent of the parties:

    A. To provide high quality library services to the public at large and to the faculty and students of the College.

    B. To maximize the use of funds and facilities for libraries and avoid unnecessary duplication of facilities and services.

    C. To jointly provide programs and facilities that are better than either entity could provide on its own.

D. To further the relationship between College and the community.
E. To provide students and faculty of the College with access to the larger holdings of the Library.
F. To provide the citizens of St. Lucie County with access to the electronic resources of the College.

II. ROLE OF THE PARTIES

In consideration of mutual covenants and promises herein contained, Trustees and County agree as follows:

A. County agrees to provide funds to Trustees in the amount of $_____ for the purchase of equipment, shelving, books, subscriptions, audiovisual resources, supplies, utilities, and support one full-time staff position including benefits. The 1994-1995 budget to accomplish these ends is attached and hereto referred to as Exhibit A. For fiscal year 1995-96, County agrees to provide funds to Trustees in the amount of $_____ for the purchase of books, subscriptions, audiovisual resources, supplies, utilities, and additional funding to support one full-time staff position including benefits.
B. For future fiscal years, the parties agree to meet on or before February 1 of each fiscal year beginning February 1, 1996 to confer and develop a proposed operating budget. Trustees agree to provide County within ninety (90) days following the end of each fiscal year evidence of expended funds provided and receipts supporting those expenditures.
C. County agrees that the responsibility for the administration of the shared resources center rests with the College's Learning Resources Director.
D. County and Trustees agree that a joint liaison committee will be established consisting of representatives of the two institutions to examine the shared resources operation and advise the Director on budget, acquisitions, and other aspects of the joint use library operation.
E. Trustees agree that equipment and maintenance thereof will be the responsibility of the Trustees except that County will be responsible for the SIRSI on-line catalog terminals and peripherals.
F. Trustees agree to inventory and advise County of any and all library materials, equipment and furnishing purchased with County funds. Trustees agree that County will control the selection and purchase of books and materials by County for the library.

G. Trustees will house within existing library facility mutually agreed upon collections or newly purchased library materials that County deems necessary to support the residents of County.

H. Trustees and County agree to provide reciprocal borrowing for residents of St. Lucie County and the faculty and students of the College.

I. Trustees agree to circulate County's library materials on County's circulation system.

J. Trustees agree to provide County access to the College's electronic resources.

K. Trustees and County will mutually agree upon a wiring infrastructure that will accommodate the library automation systems in use at the St. Lucie West library facility.

L. Trustees agree to be responsible for damages to County's designated equipment and to give proper notification to County when equipment needs normal maintenance or basic service occurring during the periods County's designated equipment is used by Trustees.

M. When fully operational, Trustees agree to open the library for public use during the following minimum hours: Monday through Friday 9:00 a.m.-5:00 p.m.; two nights each week until 8:00 p.m. and from 9:00 a.m.-12:00 p.m. on each Saturday.

N. In the event of discontinuance of funding by the Florida Legislature in subsequent years, or the termination of this contract, the SIRSI library system and rental book collection shall revert to County. All other items shall become the property of Trustees.

O. County agrees that Florida Atlantic University will participate in the shared resources center. All parties participating agree to the conditions necessary to maximize access to the information resources provided by each institution.

III. TERM; TERMINATION

This Agreement shall be effective for a period of twenty (20) years beginning July 1, 1995; provided, however, that either party may elect to terminate the agreement with or without cause on 120 days written notice of said termination. Funds involved in said agreement shall be prorated through the date of termination.

IV. AMENDMENT

This agreement may be amended by written agreement of the parties.

V. NOTICES

All notices, requests, consents, and other communications required or permitted under this Agreement shall be in writing (including telex and telegraphic communication) and shall be (as elected by the person giving such notice) hand delivered by messenger or courier service, telecommunicated, or mailed (airmail if international) by registered or certified mail (postage prepaid), return receipt requested, and addressed to:

As to St. Lucie County:	With a copy to:
St. Lucie County Administrator	St. Lucie County Attorney
2300 Virginia Avenue	2300 Virginia Avenue
Administration Annex	Administration Annex
Fort Pierce, Florida 34982	Fort Pierce, Florida 34982

As to Trustees:	With a copy to:
President	IRCC Board of Trustees Attorney
Indian River Community College	311 South Second Street
3209 Virginia Avenue	Fort Pierce, Florida 34950
Fort Pierce, Florida 34982-5596	

or to such other address as any party may designate by notice complying with the terms of this Section. Each such notice shall be deemed delivered: (a) on the date delivered if by personal delivery, (b) on the date telecommunicated if by telegraph, (c) on the date of transmission with confirmed answer back if by telex, and (d) on the date upon which the return receipt is signed or delivery is refused or the notice is designated by the postal authorities as not deliverable, as the case may be, if mailed.

VI. AUDIT

The parties agrees that either party or any of its duly authorized representatives shall, until the expiration of five (5) years after expenditure of funds under this Agreement, have access to and the right to examine any directly pertinent books, documents, papers, and records of the other party involving transactions related to this Agreement.

VII. PUBLIC RECORDS

The parties shall allow public access to all documents, papers, letters, or other materials subject to the provisions of Chapter 119, Florida Statutes, and made or received by either party in conjunction with this Agreement.

VIII. ASSIGNMENT

No party shall assign this Agreement to any other persons or firm without first obtaining the non assigning parties' approval.

IX. WHOLE UNDERSTANDING

This Agreement embodies the whole understanding of the parties. There are no promises, terms, conditions, or obligations other than those contained herein, and this Agreement shall supersede all previous communications, representations, or agreements, either verbal or written, between the parties hereto.

IN WITNESS WHEREOF, the parties have caused the execution by their duly authorized officials as of the date aforesaid.

Seminole Community Library: Joint-Use Library Services for the Community and the College

James Olliver
Susan Anderson

SUMMARY. St. Petersburg College and the City of Seminole in Pinellas County, Florida have entered into an agreement to build a joint-use library to serve both the city and the college. The library is being constructed on the Seminole Campus of the college, a new campus, and completion is planned for Fall 2003. The library will be managed and staffed by the city, while the college owns the building and provides administrative support functions (e.g., technical support, maintenance, and

James Olliver is Provost, Seminole Campus and eCampus, St. Petersburg College. He is responsible for academic and administrative programs and services as well as community relations. He is the author of a number of publications and presentations, the most recent on "Creating A Model E-Campus: Sharing Practical Solutions and Lessons Learned" at the 2001 League for Innovation Conference on Information Technology.

Susan Anderson is Library Director, St. Petersburg College. Her interest in joint-use libraries dates to her 1988 dissertation at Nova Southeastern University on joint-use libraries in Florida.

Address correspondence to: Dr. James Olliver, Provost, Seminole Campus, St. Petersburg College, 9200 113th Street North, Seminole, FL 33772 (E-mail: olliverj@ spcollege.edu) or Dr. Susan Anderson, Director of Libraries, St. Petersburg College, 7200 66th Street North, Pinellas Park, FL 33781 (E-mail: andersons@spjc.edu).

[Haworth co-indexing entry note]: "Seminole Community Library: Joint-Use Library Services for the Community and the College." Olliver, James, and Susan Anderson. Co-published simultaneously in *Resource Sharing & Information Networks* (The Haworth Information Press, an imprint of The Haworth Press, Inc.) Vol. 15, No. 1/2, 2001, pp. 89-102; and: *Joint-Use Libraries* (ed: William Miller, and Rita M. Pellen) The Haworth Information Press, an imprint of The Haworth Press, Inc., 2001, pp. 89-102. Single or multiple copies of this article are available for a fee from The Haworth Document Delivery Service [1-800-HAWORTH, 9:00 a.m. - 5:00 p.m. (EST). E-mail address: getinfo@haworthpress.com].

security). This library is one of a number of joint-use libraries operating or planned in Florida. *[Article copies available for a fee from The Haworth Document Delivery Service: 1-800-HAWORTH. E-mail address: <getinfo@haworthpress. com> Website: <http://www.HaworthPress.com> © 2001 by The Haworth Press, Inc. All rights reserved.]*

KEYWORDS. Joint-use library, partnerships, community

St. Petersburg College and the City of Seminole, FL are about to open a new joint-use library, which will be the fourth building on a new campus of the college. Even though the city already has a library near this site, possibilities for growth were limited and the city would like to serve college students at the new campus as well as its more traditional constituencies. For the college, joining with the public library enables it to jump-start the traditional collection and staffing needs, while at the same time helping to fulfill its mission of deep involvement with the surrounding community. Together, the city and the college are building a library with resources neither could have afforded on its own, and which will serve all constituencies from childhood to old age with seamless library services. It took nearly two years of planning and work to develop the proposal for the joint-use library. After approval by city council and the college governing board, an eighteen-month construction project began. The building is two-story, clearly visible from a major north south roadway. The expected completion date for the joint-use library is August 2003.

A FIRST STEP ON THE PATH

Almost from the initial meeting of the Seminole City Council where St. Petersburg College President, Carl M. Kuttler, announced the College's plans for construction of the Seminole Campus, college and city officials perceived the wisdom of a joint-use library facility. A goal of the college is to further its integration with the community. The vision for the new campus was not "we" and "they." It was "us." Every step of planning had involvement from both the city perspective and the college perspective.

The Seminole Campus, which opened its first building in 1998, was a new campus with no library resources. As planning groups began to talk about the campus, it was soon apparent that the existing public library located directly across the street from the campus could serve and has served as an interim library for print resources for the campus. The idea of a new library for the city was welcomed because the city library was rapidly outgrowing its space. Once that first step was taken, ideas began to form about a larger, expanded library to serve both the community and the college.

A joint-use library for the Seminole Campus of St. Petersburg College is not a new concept in terms of library service. There are numerous examples of joint-use libraries. But for the citizens of Seminole, a small city in the heart of Pinellas County, this was a new and challenging idea. For the college it was another opportunity for cooperation and partnership, for which the college is known.

The city of Seminole has about 17,000 residents, but the greater Seminole area of the county, an unincorporated area, has about 90,000 residents and is growing. The city of Seminole has been traditionally a retirement community, but its current and expected growth is in younger families. Pinellas County, where the city is located, is the most densely populated county in Florida with a population approaching 900,000.

THE EXISTING PATH: SEMINOLE CITY LIBRARY

The current community library is only eight years old and community residents are very proud of their "new" library which replaced a very small, approximately 3,000 square foot library staffed primarily by volunteers. It was a major decision for the city to form a "real" library. The result has been successful beyond expectations and now the "new" library needed to be expanded or moved.

After only a few years of operation the community library was at capacity. The building has 17,500 square feet and three large meeting rooms. Children's programs were very successful and the space for children's services was too small. In the stacks, books were already being piled on the floor. When expansion of the current building was investigated by the architectural firm that designed the building, they found that the building could be expanded in only a very limited way. The library could be added on to on the east or the north but the constraints of the lot meant that only about 8,000 square feet could be added at an estimated cost of $1.6 million. The building was not designed to support a second floor. No city funds had been planned for such an expansion.

The issue of tax increases which might be needed to support additional library services, not just for city residents but also for the growing numbers of residents in the unincorporated areas, was of major concern.

However, the city is not the sole support of library services. The county-wide library cooperative collects millage based on the number of residents from unincorporated areas using each city library and applies a formula to redistribute funds. Those funds are never the full cost of library service for the cities.

THE NEW PATH:
SEMINOLE CAMPUS, ST. PETERSBURG COLLEGE

St. Petersburg Jr. College has owned the 100+ acres of grove and wetlands on the west side of 113th Street for over 30 years in anticipation of population growth which would require a campus in that area of the county. The campus is located directly across the street from the community library and the community post office.

When the college opened the campus to the first class of students in the fall of 1998 there was one building but many cooperative arrangements. Previously, classes were taught in the city recreation center on the south side of the campus. Traditional library services, such as print reference sources, were provided by the community library.

Students registered at any campus have remote access to electronic resources and only electronic library services were planned for the initial phase of the Seminole Campus. The state of Florida, through the Distance Learning Library Initiative, DLLI, provides access to databases and to electronic encyclopedias. The college provides access to proprietary library databases and the library catalog through the library Website, "The Library Online." Students can search the collections of any campus of the college and have books sent to the Seminole campus for their use. The college libraries use document delivery software to scan and fax or e-mail non-returnable library materials between campus libraries. The college offers both an online and traditional information literacy course. Additionally, the college requires that students demonstrate computer and information literacy competencies during the first twelve hours of enrollment and prior to taking online courses. These competencies can be achieved by enrolling in specified courses such as Computer and Information Literacy or by passing an online test for those competencies. Although these efforts insure good access to library resources, reference services and print reference materials were still needed to support courses.

The close proximity of the Seminole Community Library seemed a good solution to providing these services. Very early in the planning stages of the Seminole Campus, city officials and community library staff were approached by college staff with the request to provide these library services to students. A committee of college and city staff was formed–the Library Resources Committee. The response from the city was very positive and even before the campus opened, the community library was offering services for college students.

A CAUTIOUS STEP FORWARD:
ISSUES FOR PLANNING A JOINT-USE LIBRARY

The major issue in establishing a joint-use library is in determining the mission or missions of the libraries considering a merger. If the missions of the libraries have common goals the project has a chance for success. Public libraries pride themselves on providing free service to all citizens, but some academic institutions serve only students and faculty. Many librarians believe that each type of library has a different mission and a different clientele who should not intermingle. College students and children should never occupy the same building according to some professionals.

According to Lynch's *The Librarian's Guide to Partnerships*, "Each organization has its own structure, traditions, and operating style. Partners who intend to operate a joint facility must be willing to learn and respect what is important to each other, what is expected and valued by the members of each organization and how they operate on a daily basis."

An inter-agency agreement or contract must be negotiated. Some libraries have very detailed and specific contracts. Others have only general terms. The daily operation of a joint-use library is critical to its success. The operational agreement, which may or may not be part of a more global agreement, must address issues such as the calendar of operation, hours of operation, and schedules of employees. The working calendar of the public library and academic library are different. Collection maintenance and development is another issue since many public libraries keep only those items with high circulation while academic libraries rarely rely on circulation statistics to determine whether to add and keep a title. The classification system can be another difficult issue. It is often necessary for one library to reclassify materials to a different classification scheme. Library instruction is a major service provided by academic libraries and is increasingly of interest to public libraries. The responsibilities of the librarians in this area must be specified. The responsibility for purchase, maintenance, and replacement of equipment and furnishings must be part of a written document.

The library building design is a major consideration in providing services to different patron groups. Quiet study must be balanced with children's programming. Library instruction spaces must be balanced with the need for meeting rooms. Service points such as circulation and reference must be equally available for all users.

Public users require wheelchair and stroller-convenient parking adjacent to the building. A good plan is to provide identified parking for the community users of the joint library.

THE NEXT STEP DOWN THE PATH:
THE SEMINOLE JOINT-USE LIBRARY PROJECT BEGINS

The next step in the project was to learn about other joint-use libraries. A Joint-Use Subcommittee of the Library Resources Committee was formed which included the mayor of Seminole. Documents, agreements, floor plans and articles from other joint-use library projects were obtained and studied. The statewide community college library automation system for Florida, The College Center for Library Automation (CCLA), has a number of advisory committees. One of these committees focuses on joint-use library projects. The CCLA planning document, "Issues Related to the Establishment of Joint-Use Libraries," helped guide the committee as it studied the feasibility of the combined libraries.

Members of the committee traveled to Broward County, Florida to see joint-use libraries in operation. Broward Community College shares three campus libraries. Two of the libraries are large regional joint-use libraries with the Broward County Public Library. On the central campus of the college, the library is a joint-use facility with Florida Atlantic University. A campus of the university adjoins the college campus. These are well-known and very successful examples of joint-use library service.

Library consultant, Dr. Ruth O'Donnell, was hired by the city to study the Seminole joint-use project. Dr. O'Donnell interviewed city and college staff, reviewed documents and concluded: "The city should make this offer to SPJC [St. Petersburg Junior College, now called St. Petersburg College] based on future library needs. The consultant suggests the need for a larger library is already evident and will increase and that the city will be addressing library space needs again, on its own, if it does not act not to join with SPJC to maximize resources for community library service. The offer to share costs for a library is a very good opportunity for the residents of Seminole."

With Dr. O'Donnell's report in hand the staff of the city began working to develop a concrete proposal to present to the college based on no new taxes. The City Manager worked with the City Library Director to estimate the value of the current library collections and resources and possible grant funding. The report included a section on the costs to re-model the current library and add approximately 8,000 square feet.

The college used this time to have architectural concept drawings completed which showed a possible exterior of a new building, site location and possible floor plans. These concept drawings incorporated the services that the staffs of the city library and the college had determined to be necessary in a joint-use facility. The concept drawings showed a possible two-story building which would include a café or food court, Friends offices and sales areas, children's programming areas, meeting and conference rooms, quiet study and reading areas, electronic resources areas or information commons, traditional stacks, a gallery area, and classrooms.

After reviewing the feasibility report of the City Manager and the concept drawings, the city decided to hold three public forums for community input. Following these forums, the City Council planned to vote on the proposal.

The opinions expressed at the public forums were almost evenly divided between those favoring the project and those against it. These forums gave citizens the opportunity to express their concerns which ranged from older residents who worried about losing the community "feel" of the library to parents who wanted improved library services as they planned for the future educational needs of their children.

The Seminole City Council met on November 24, 1998 for a vote, but decided to postpone the vote until the city manager completed one further task. The Council asked for a cost estimate to convert the current library to a new City Hall and the cost to re-convert the current City Hall to a public works building. On December 8 the city manager presented his report including architectural sketches and cost estimates for conversion of the buildings. The City Council then voted to send the proposal to the college. There was one negative vote cast by a City Council member who has consistently objected to the project.

The following Monday, the Board of Trustees of St. Petersburg Junior College met for a workshop to consider the proposal. Later, in the formal Board meeting, the proposal was approved. Trustee Lacy Harwell said: "This is a splendid symbol of the cooperation everyone is going to have to exhibit in the coming century."

A CREATIVE JOURNEY: DESIGNING THE BUILDING

In making a decision to go forward with the project, it was important for the city to maintain and expand established successful services and programs. Essential needs were to expand public access to computers and databases, and to provide additional space for children's and young adult programming and services.

In an article in *The Encyclopedia of Library and Information Science*, I. S. "Bud" Call remarks:

> . . . the desired outcome is that by combining the resources available from two or more agencies or institutions and sharing the operational costs, the patrons from each of the parties involved will have access to more library materials and services at little or no additional expense to each of the partners involved in the agreement. The only significant disadvantage to a joint-use library agreement is the adjustment that each of the partners has to make in becoming sensitive to the needs of the others. Decisions and policies can no longer reflect only the needs of one or the other, but must be made in accordance with the combined needs of both. A joint-use library is totally unique unto itself and must always be treated as such.

The college campus needed a multi-functional building that included classrooms, faculty offices, food services and other amenities in addition to a campus library. The multipurpose nature of the building is important because it matches the approach taken in other Campus buildings which are multi-functional and because it makes a statement about the Seminole Campus approach to library services. While the campus philosophy may not be traditional in its approach, Seminole faculty and administrators understand and support the key role librarians can have in assisting students/patrons. The addition of a multi-purpose building with a highly visible library function underscores the importance of the role of librarians in both the finding, and, more importantly, the evaluation of information once identified.

The second issue of major importance to the campus and to the city was that the building be a community building. Having children and teens on campus lets them (and their parents) gain a familiarity with the campus community and see the college as a logical and preferred choice for post-secondary education. An important space need of the city was room for community meetings. The final plan of the building has three "community rooms" that can be connected into one large community room. Community rooms are used for everything from tax preparation seminars for senior citizens to children's story time, and are available for the college's use as well.

The third issue of major importance to the campus, the college and the city was to provide the library services and resources of a traditional library building providing an environment conducive to individual and collaborative learning. Although the building is designed with high-speed networks, computer classrooms, and a considerable number of computers for students/patrons to use for research and communications, the new building does not accentuate technology and its uses as do the earlier campus buildings. The substantial number of books and periodicals provided by the city through existing collections complements the high tech infrastructure to create a traditional atmosphere and environment with a technology backbone. Through cooperation with the city, the joint-use library provides the new campus with the benefits of a traditional library environment including reference services, stacks, comfortable sitting for leisurely reading, quiet study rooms and other services without incurring the cost of developing an initial campus collection or full library staff.

Through an extended process of give and take, both parties achieved their major objectives in the building design without feeling their autonomy was compromised. Early in the discussions about the library, and especially during the public hearings held by the Seminole City Council, there were serious concerns raised about the loss of autonomy by the city. Residents feared that the college would overtake "our little library." The college worked very hard throughout these discussions and the detailed design work to make this a true partnership. If there is a common goal of community service, issues of autonomy and control tend to be a very secondary concern.

A small café included in the building is envisioned as a community meeting place providing coffee and conversation, space to enjoy reading a newspaper, or even do a little e-mail in a comfortable atmosphere. Food service will be provided by a vendor. The goal is to provide limited food service for the community library users and the students in a setting that will encourage use of the building and its resources.

Architecturally the building mirrors the glazes, large expanses of glass, and same roofing look of the first two buildings. The look has been called "Floribbean." It is located for easy access by the public with parking immediately adjacent. It connects to the campus through walkways. The large window walls have views of the environmentally protected wetlands of the campus.

THE PATHWAY WIDENS: SEMINOLE CAMPUS GROWS

The Seminole Campus has been called the "Technology Campus" of the college, not so much for having so many technology classes but because the campus philosophy is to look for a technological solution first, and then rely on traditional approaches to education. This means online student services, extensive use of technology in classes, and expectations that faculty and staff will take advantage of technology tools. In the area of library services: "The primary library resources provided for the Seminole students and faculty are electronic. As the home of eCampus, the Seminole library is expected to look at electronic resources that would be useful for both face-to-face and e-courses. Reference materials and online materials and databases have greater priority for purchasing than at the other campus libraries" (*St. Petersburg College Campus Library Material Expenditure Plan, 2002-2003*).

The first building on the campus housed an information commons. The entire building is 24,000 square feet and 6,000 square feet of that is a multi-purpose room meant to serve students for electronic library resources, registration, financial aid, remediation, testing and coursework; and to serve faculty as a development center for new courses and new teaching methods. The first courses planned for the Seminole Campus were general education.

The second and third buildings are a maintenance/facilities/storage building and the three-story University Partnership Center (UPC). At more than 86,000 square feet, the UPC is the largest building ever constructed at St. Petersburg College. A multipurpose building designed to serve the increasingly diverse needs of a growing Campus, the UPC Building includes unique spaces, but the heart and soul of the building might best be described as classrooms, classrooms, and more classrooms–with 28 specialized and general-purpose learning spaces located on three floors. The building extends the design concept of multipurpose use of space, so successful in the first building, to the new UPC.

The University Partnership Building is the home of a growing number of educational partnerships that offer Pinellas County residents the opportunity to earn undergraduate and graduate degrees. The partnerships, currently with fourteen colleges and universities, are unique in that the partnering institutions teach the courses and award the degrees, but the classes are held at St. Petersburg College. For example, the latest effort allows students to receive a Doctor of Pharmacy degree from the University of Florida while remaining in Pinellas County.

In the UPC building is the first auditorium facility in Pinellas County with live cable broadcast and Webcast capabilities. The Digital Auditorium ("digitorium") integrates two major communication tools–computers and the television. Instructors, students and staff have access to a state-of-the-art learning facility equipped with the latest in digital video and Web presentation equipment and capabilities. Individuals or small groups can make presentations to be shown "live" throughout the world on the Internet (via Webcasts) or recorded for later distribution on the net through streaming video or other media. The venue serves as a new kind of theater for video concerts, lectures and other presentations displayed on two 10' 6" × 14' screens. The facility is capable of receiving satellite downlinks. The facility can also be used for the traditional purpose of teaching traditional classes, making community presentations, or holding other types of meetings. The "digitorium" is unique in form as well as function. It is designed as a 200-seat facility, but four classrooms of 40 seats each can be opened to view auditorium presentations, giving a capacity for 360 seats. The 40 seat classrooms serve as "breakout" rooms.

The fourth building for the Seminole Campus is the new joint-use library, "The Seminole Community Library at Seminole Campus, St. Petersburg College."

THE VIEW DOWN THE PATH:
BENEFITS OF THE SEMINOLE JOINT-USE LIBRARY

The library will provide a seasoned staff to serve the expanded facility. Both the college and city are adding dollars to increase the library hours from the current 52 hours per week to 73.5 hours per week, but the core staff will remain the city library staff who have served the community so well. During the public hearings held prior to the joint venture being approved, the fact that existing staff would be providing service in the new facility won over a lot of people who were concerned about losing the values and attributes of a "community library" they so very much appreciated.

Anderson, in "Planning for Joint Use Libraries" (*Florida Libraries* 42:7), says, "The benefits of a joint-use library are the reasons that communities are willing to deal with the complexities of a joint venture. Probably the most important benefit is an increase in library service and resources for the participating groups."

The new library will be larger and add extra features and functions not available in the current library. A key ingredient for both parties is the extras in the new building which are not available in the current library, for example, the café, quiet study rooms, a teen room for the city, class and conference rooms for the college, and a separate area for The Friends of the Library. Of equal importance was the expansion of some existing spaces, including more books and reading areas, a much enlarged children's area, and many more powerful computers connected to a high speed network. The library service area in the new facility will be more than double existing library space.

The library provides spaces that support both the college's and the city's objectives. Earlier in this article we commented about the goals each party has for the new facility. By combining efforts several areas on both "lists" were funded which couldn't have happened separately. Some areas, like the proposed café, might not have been successful without the "critical mass" brought by the combined "traffic" of both parties.

The library melds the "traditional" and the electronic. The existing books, periodicals, videos, stacks, and even some furniture and fixtures moved from the current facility to the new one will give the library a familiarity and warmth patrons have come to expect and appreciate. At the same time, the library will be equipped with 50 open access computers, all with high-speed access to the Internet. There will be wireless capability throughout the building as well.

The library builds on the strengths and contributions of each party. The city will contribute its existing collection, furniture, fixtures and equipment, having an approximate value of a million dollars, to the new facility. The College will provide its expertise in construction management and technical support, and will cover the costs of maintenance, custodial, security and related facilities functions.

WALKING TOGETHER: OPERATING THE JOINT-USE LIBRARY

Each library in the partnership gave up a certain amount of autonomy or control to achieve the benefits of cooperation. Many of these issues surfaced in the crafting of the formal agreement between the parties, and others arose as the square footage in the building was planned. Still more will no doubt arise as a series of "understandings" related to the operational aspects of the partnership not included in the formal agreement are written.

The College owns the building, and, as such, has certain responsibilities in law and procedure that it will need to maintain. These responsibilities vary from maintenance staff ratios to the location of exit doors, accessibility and other issues.

The responsibility for the daily management of the library is with the city. The Seminole Community Library Director will manage the library. A "professional-in-charge" who currently oversees the campus' two computer commons will serve as the primary point person for library services and liaison between the campus and the city. The college library director will confer with the city library director and the liaison on college-wide library issues. Operational guidelines or understandings are being drafted to assist in the running of the library.

The college library director will ensure that the new library policies and procedures are compatible with those of the other campus libraries and that services and resources between campuses are seamless. The college provides the library automation and library management system for the joint library. In preparation for the transition, the community library data records were extracted from the previous automation system and have been merged with records from the other campus libraries. This extraction and migration included all bibliographic and patron records. The community library began using the college library automation system in fall 2001.

The college will migrate to the state funded library automation system designed to serve all of the community colleges and state universities in Florida. This change is anticipated for mid-winter 2003-04. In preparation, the college library inventoried all collections including the community library collection.

Many other issues arise in a joint venture. For example, the city library uses a different book security system from the college library system. A decision was made to change the city system to the college system. The city library collections will receive new security stripping prior to the move to the new building.

THE VIEW AT THE END OF THE PATH:
A CENTER FOR COMMUNITY SERVICES AND RESOURCES

The city plans for the Seminole City Hall to move into the space occupied by the current city library when the joint-use library opens. The new joint-use facility will be right in the middle of an area which includes the campus, City Hall, the post office and the city recreation center. The Greater Seminole Area Chamber of Commerce is located just down the street. This geographic proximity provides a hub for educational, recreational, civic and business activity for the Greater Seminole Area.

WE FIND OUR WAY: CONCLUSION

Joint-use libraries are certainly an option for communities to consider. "Just how good are joint-use libraries? They're as good as we make them," said I. S. "Bud" Call ("Joint-use Libraries: Just How Good Are They?" *College and Research Libraries News*, November 1993).

Strong arguments can be made for efficiency and cost savings. Strong arguments can be made that the libraries will lose unique qualities. With careful planning the quantity and quality of services and materials can be dramatically increased for both libraries. This does not mean that a joint-use library is the right choice for every community, but it is the right choice for the city of Seminole and St. Petersburg College. The population of the city was expanding beyond what current library services could meet, and a campus library would have been built very near the public library, so combining resources and facilities was a reasonable option. The *St. Petersburg Times* reported "the decision is whether to take a leap of faith." This cooperative project between the city of Seminole and St. Petersburg College reinforces the concept that St. Petersburg College is a "community college," that Seminole Campus is a "community campus," and the joint library will be a "community library."

REFERENCES

Anderson, Susan. "Planning for Joint Use Libraries." *Florida Libraries* 42:7 November/December 1999, 109-115.

Call, I. S. "Bud." "Joint-Use Libraries: Just How Good Are They?" *College and Research Libraries News*, November 1993, 551-556.

Call, I. S. "Bud." "Joint-Use Libraries: The Issues." *Encyclopedia of Library and Information Science* (New York: Marcel Dekker, 1997).

College Center for Library Automation. "Issues Related to the Establishment of Joint-Use Libraries," *College Center for Library Automation, Standing Committee on Joint-Use Libraries,* January 30, 1996.

Lynch, Sherry, editor. *The Librarian's Guide to Partnerships, Highsmith Press Handbook Series,* (Ft. Atkinson, Wisconsin: Highsmith Press, 1999).

O'Donnell, Ruth. "Feasibility Review of a Joint Use Library: City of Seminole Florida and St. Petersburg Junior College," (June 30 1998), 24.

M. M. Bennett Library, St. Petersburg College, Campus Library Expenditure Plan, 2002/03.

Marshall, Janet. "Library Decision Is Due Today." *St. Petersburg Times, Seminole Times,* December 8, 1998, 1.

Joint-Use Libraries:
Balancing Autonomy and Cooperation

Karen A. Dornseif

SUMMARY. Harmony Library in Fort Collins, Colorado, is a joint-use library built and operated by Front Range Community College and the City of Fort Collins. In planning this library, the partners carefully crafted a common vision and then examined their own libraries and expectations, identifying the areas in which they needed to maintain control and those in which they could operate less independently. Using examples from over four years of experience at Harmony Library, the author shows how balancing the need for control with the opportunities for cooperation is an ongoing, delicate process enhanced by constant communication and coordination. *[Article copies available for a fee from The Haworth Document Delivery Service: 1-800-HAWORTH. E-mail address: <getinfo@haworthpress.com> Website: <http://www.HaworthPress.com> © 2001 by The Haworth Press, Inc. All rights reserved.]*

KEYWORDS. Joint-use libraries, community college libraries, public libraries, Colorado, community colleges

INTRODUCTION

Joint-use libraries are successful when the patrons of each partner believe that the library functions well for them. Partnerships must be en-

---

Karen A. Dornseif is Campus Librarian, Harmony Library, Front Range Community College/Larimer Campus, Fort Collins, CO 80526-3812 (E-mail: kdornseif@larimer.cccoes.edu).

[Haworth co-indexing entry note]: "Joint-Use Libraries: Balancing Autonomy and Cooperation." Dornseif, Karen A. Co-published simultaneously in *Resource Sharing & Information Networks* (The Haworth Information Press, an imprint of The Haworth Press, Inc.) Vol. 15, No. 1/2, 2001, pp. 103-115; and: *Joint-Use Libraries* (ed: William Miller, and Rita M. Pellen) The Haworth Information Press, an imprint of The Haworth Press, Inc., 2001, pp. 103-115. Single or multiple copies of this article are available for a fee from The Haworth Document Delivery Service [1-800-HAWORTH, 9:00 a.m. - 5:00 p.m. (EST). E-mail address: getinfo@haworthpress.com].

http://www.haworthpress.com/store/product.asp?sku=J121
© 2001 by The Haworth Press, Inc. All rights reserved.
10.1300/J121v15n01_08

tered into with enthusiasm, a high level of trust between all of the participants, extensive knowledge of each library's mission and patrons, and a willingness to critically examine assumptions and traditions and create solutions with flexibility and grace.

There is no model joint-use library. Each reflects not only the institutional culture, mission, and circumstances of every partner, but the unique combination of these in a shared facility.

Whatever the arrangement, partnering in a joint-use library is a balancing act. Balancing the need for autonomy with the cooperation needed to achieve benefits begins in the earliest stages of planning and will continue throughout the life of the joint-use library.

BACKGROUND

In 1995, the Larimer Campus of Front Range Community College in Fort Collins, Colorado, was providing library services to a student body of 1,900 FTE in a 1,600 square foot facility with a minimal collection of materials. The staff consisted of a campus librarian and various part-time, temporary employees and work-study students.

The Fort Collins Public Library was struggling to serve a community rapidly growing toward 100,000 people from a 35,000 square foot facility in downtown Fort Collins, about six miles north of the FRCC campus. After an initial attempt to construct a small joint-use library on the campus failed, the public library in July 1995 opened a Mini-Library branch about two miles from the campus.

Responding to clear evidence of need for an adequate library on the Larimer Campus, the Colorado legislature included funding in its FY1996 budget to plan and build a 19,000 square foot college library. No additional funds were allocated for operations or materials. With an eye toward combining resources with the city, the college engaged an architectural firm to develop the program plan for a college library as required by the state governing board. While this program plan was being developed with stakeholders from both the college and community, the director of the Fort Collins Public Library developed a proposal for city funding to supplement the college's state allocation for construction and for operation of a joint-use library.

Representatives of the college and the city negotiated an agreement to structure the construction and operation of the proposed joint-use library. By early 1996 the funding was secured, the governing document was completed and signed by all parties, an amended program plan for a joint-use library was accepted and approved by the state, and the design of the library proceeded. A broad range of representatives of the two partners in the endeavor wielded shovels at the groundbreaking in September 1996. Construction began in early 1997, and Harmony Library opened on January 31, 1998.

As the campus librarian, I have been involved with the project from its inception, and continue as co-manager of Harmony Library. The campus vice-president, the public library director and her supervisor, the city's director of cultural, library and recreation services, and the public library's branch manager at Harmony Library have moved on and been replaced with others who were not involved in the initial planning of the facility.

Many of the examples provided below reflect our experiences at Harmony Library. In our early stages of development, we relied heavily on the existing body of literature on joint-use libraries and what we learned from visits to public/community college libraries in Broward County, Florida. We continue to evolve, learning from our own successes and failures and the questions of librarians who are dreaming of, planning, building or operating their own unique joint-use libraries.

THE VISION

Before the would-be partners in a joint-use library decide what automation system to use, who pays the electricity bill, or how broken furniture is replaced, they must arrive at a common vision for the new library. This statement of the partners' aspirations and expectations will establish the foundation for the partnership, underlying negotiations and their relationship from that point forward.

An important question to address in guiding this discussion is what the partners hope to achieve by combining resources (Schwanz 2000), to whatever extent that will be. This is an opportunity to let imaginations soar. Reality will hit soon enough.

AUTONOMY

If autonomy means independence in the most absolute sense, our experience shows that there is none in a joint-use library. *Every* decision made by one partner impacts the partnership library. The partners do, however, maintain some level of control in some areas. When the partners share a vision, they should be able to examine their own libraries and identify those areas where they cannot yield control in a joint-use endeavor.

The following are areas where both the public and college libraries at Harmony Library maintain autonomy:

Identity

We describe Harmony Library as both a college library and a public library to assure our separate patron groups that Harmony Library is their library.

Mission

Our separate missions remain intact, incorporated in Harmony's mission statement.

Ownership of Materials

Sitting side by side on the shelves, our materials are clearly identified as belonging to either the public or college library.

Bibliographic Records

We each own our bibliographic records.

Collection Development

Each library selects materials for the common collection according to its own collection development policy.

Materials Challenges

Challenges to materials are handled by the owning library according to its own policies.

Internal Relationships

We respect and accommodate the internal chains of command of and obligations to the parent organizations.

External Relationships

Both libraries maintain memberships in external consortia, systems and organizations that reflect their specific needs.

Many libraries in joint-use endeavors identify other areas as those in which they will maintain control and independence. These include retaining a classification system that is different from that of the partner library, shelving collections separately, retaining a separate library card for their users, and maintaining circulation policies adapted to distinct groups of users.

CONTINUUM OF INTEGRATION

Ideally, joint-use libraries would decide how extensively they will integrate collections, operations, services and resources based on what would be best for the combined patrons of the joint-use library, but these decisions are often driven by each library's need for autonomy. Along a continuum of integration of resources, operations and management, libraries may choose–

Minimal Integration

Large, well-established libraries generally choose this model, primarily because it is too difficult and costly to dismantle what exists and has been working. The most common example of minimal integration is two libraries merely sharing a building.

Selective Integration

One variation involves dividing responsibilities among the partners, building on existing strengths and specialties. For example, the academic partner would provide the reference collection and information services while the public library provides circulation services and popular materials.

Another variation is based on the specific needs and use patterns of the patrons. In some school/public combinations, the school library operates the joint-use library for its students during the day while the public library staffs the library in the evenings and during the summer.

Full Integration

In this type of joint-use library, the missions of the two partner libraries are merged into a unifying mission for the joint-use library. Staffs are combined, trained and managed to serve all library patrons, materials are integrated on the shelves and in the catalog and available to all patrons, and all areas of the library are open to all users. This type of joint-use library operates with common policies and procedures. We describe Harmony Library as fully integrated, with only minor exceptions, such as college reserves being available only to FRCC students.

AGREEING ON BASICS

Once the foundation is laid with a solid statement of intentions, identification of the areas where the partners must maintain control, and a choice of a level of integration, the partners must address the specifics of how the library will be constructed and operated. This articulation of the rights and obligation of the partners is variously called a Memorandum of Agreement, an Inter-Institutional Agreement or, in the case of Harmony Library, an Intergovernmental Agreement.

Some basic decisions will involve the following:

Location

Each partner in a joint-use library wants the library to be in the most convenient location for its users, the decision heavily influenced by land cost and availability. Most colleges and schools will want their library on the campus. Public library choices are influenced by population patterns, accessibility from major traffic arteries and visibility. Harmony Library is located at the west end of our campus, the first building along a campus road leading from a major city street. The campus is in the southern part of Fort Collins, an area of rapid population growth.

Ownership

Who owns the library building? Who owns the land? The equipment, furniture and materials? When existing libraries are combined, issues arise around ownership of furniture and equipment brought into the library, that purchased as part of construction and that acquired during the life of the library.

Funding

Funding entities often envision joint-use libraries as ways to save money. While combining libraries can maximize results, all partners must fully fund their libraries to avoid compromising services. Joint-use libraries, when carefully constructed and managed, should result in "more bang for the buck" as savings accrue from lack of duplication.

In a joint-use library, the partners have to squarely address who will pay for what or how total costs will be divided. At Harmony Library, the partners agreed to a formula for construction costs based on space needs, with the college paying 60% and the city 40%. Operational cost allocations were based on anticipated use, and the city pays 60% of these.

Management and Organization

The joint-use library partners must provide for management of the library. At least three models of governance are possible (College 1996).

- One partner runs the library, employing a director. When one library contracts with another to provide the services to its patrons, this model is usually employed.
- A joint-governing board runs the library, employing a director.
- Co-directors representing the partners run the library together. In this arrangement, responsibilities may be divided, or all decisions may be jointly made. Harmony Library is jointly managed by a branch manager for the public library and the campus librarian, with each manager having primary responsibility in some areas. For example, because the college maintains the building, customer comments or complaints about room temperatures are directed to the college librarian. Complaints about circulation staff are directed to the public library manager, as the public library is primarily responsible for the day to day operation of the library.

The IGA for Harmony Library addresses management and organization in these words, "The organizational structure of the Library will be designed to meet the needs of both the City and the College, with as little duplication of services and functions as possible. Clear lines of authority and responsibility will be established consistent with this Agreement to ensure effective management of the Library" (City 1996).

The Harmony Library IGA addresses a number of other basic library elements, including:

Classification Scheme

The college agreed to convert its collection from Library of Congress to Dewey Decimal System.

Integrated Library System

The college migrated its records from CARL to the city's Dynix system, and after the city's purchase of Innovative Interfaces, Inc., to that system.

Policies and Procedures

The public library's policies and procedures are followed for the operation of the library, with exceptions made for the college as needed.

Advisory Committee

A committee of public and college representatives meets twice a year to make recommendations regarding the maintenance and operation of the library.

COOPERATION

Within joint-use libraries there are many opportunities to reap benefits through cooperation. At Harmony Library, we expected a number of advantages to combining resources, but we have been surprised at other benefits that have grown out of our partnership.

Facility

When two entities contribute to the construction or renovation of a facility, and if each entity is contributing enough to cover the cost of space for all its needs, the resulting library will be bigger, and probably nicer, than either could have provided alone. Savings accrue from lack of duplication. For example, if each entity built a library, each would have to provide a circulation desk. While the desk in a joint-use facility may be larger than in the library built by either partner, it would probably not be twice as large, and there would be only one security gate. Part of the money that both entities would have spent for the space and equipment for a circulation desk could be directed elsewhere.

Unanticipated advantages often come out of combining facilities. The small group study rooms the college planned for students at Harmony Library are used and appreciated by small groups of community members, such as neighborhood association committees and book clubs. The community meeting room funded by the public library is used for college programs and when college classes are combined for a guest speaker. The public library's children's area has been used as a lab for a children's literature class in the college's early childhood professions program.

Resources

Even when both partners continue to acquire materials according to their own collection development policies, there is enormous potential for maximizing resources available to the joint-use patrons. The purchase of basic, yet expensive, reference materials can be divided between the partners. For example, the college can justify the purchase of *McGraw-Hill's Encyclopedia for Science and Technology* that the public library couldn't justify for a branch library, while the public library updates general and medical encyclopedia sets that the college would otherwise be purchasing.

There is a surprising amount of overlap in the circulating nonfiction collection. The college is able to concentrate its buying power on more academic titles because the public library purchases some materials that are appropriate for both general public use and student research. We have found that about one fifth of the materials the college librarian selects from *Choice* reviews have already been purchased by the public library for Harmony's collection.

In the periodicals area, public library patrons appreciate having access to medical and social science journals subscribed to by the college. College instructors have built assignments around comparing coverage of a topic in professional journals and the more popular, general interest magazines subscribed to by the public library.

When Harmony Library was planned, we did not anticipate the extent to which customer needs would be met by electronic databases. A committee of public reference librarians and the campus librarian evaluates and selects databases that meet the needs of our communities. The most difficult aspect of bringing electronic databases to the joint-use library is negotiating fair subscription fees and remote access with vendors who structure fees and assign sales representatives based on types of libraries. With joint-use libraries not identified as a type, negotiating pricing and licensing is often difficult and frustrating.

Combining the programming and marketing expertise of the public library with the intellectual resources of the college opens up programming opportunities. One of the programs sponsored by the college and presented at Harmony Library has been "My Word! Readings by Writers," a series of author events. This series is coordinated by an English instructor and the campus librarian. Displays in the library advertise upcoming programs to the more than 1,000 people who come through the doors daily. In its first year, "My Word!" attracted over 400 people to five programs.

The public library's immensely successful summer reading program includes four outdoor programs that are held on a stage area near the campus student center. Students and faculty enjoy these activities with hundreds of potential students. A number of benefits grow out of our location on campus. Library staff and the library users have a cafeteria for snacks and lattes within 50 yards of the library. College public safety personnel are available to help diffuse problems with difficult customers, to transport fines and fees money to the cashier's office for deposit, to direct and manage the crowd at huge children's programs and to provide back-up when parents leave children stranded at the library at closing time.

Staffing

While the conventional wisdom cautions against combining staffs from two libraries in a joint-use library, there are advantages. Reference librarians from different types of libraries bring different expertise, knowledge and experience to their work. In the joint-use library, if staffed by both entities, that collective knowledge is a resource for all library patrons.

On the other hand, working in a joint-use library is very demanding. All patrons become primary patrons. In any desk shift, a librarian would have to be prepared to guide a college student through research for an assignment, assist a computer-phobic community patron in compiling a bibliography of titles on a hobby, help a child identify the title and status of the most recent Harry Potter book, complete a citation for a faculty member, and advise a community patron on some good historical fiction set in Ireland and involving horse racing. Reference staff can develop new skills, but the training needs are intense and continuous.

At our circulation desk, public library staff and students struggle with college reserves. It is not possible to train the large, part-time staff in all the subtleties and complexities of this collection, yet it is not heavily enough used to dedicate staff to managing and circulating it.

Work-study students supplement the circulation and shelving staffs at no cost to the library. The college's information technology department hires and manages monitors for the open computer lab available to students and the public.

BALANCING

The partners in a joint-use library must give up some control in some areas to reap the advantages of cooperation. This often involves becoming dependent on the partnering entity. Even in the least integrated of joint-use libraries, the partner libraries may have to coordinate service hours, schedule programming around one another, share parking spaces and trust the other partner to pay its fair share of the water bill.

In a highly integrated library such as Harmony, the balancing is much more complex and difficult. Enormous amounts of time and energy go into internal and external communications and coordination. Both partners, and their parent institutions, often feel frustrated at not being able to implement what seem innocuous enough changes without consulting with the other partner.

Recently, our public library determined that only new books with a publication date of 2002 would go in our highly visible new books display. The bulk of recent college purchases, published in 2001, weren't making the cutoff and being displayed with the new books. An exception for college-purchased materials was quickly implemented.

FRCC recently began a college-wide implementation of a one-card system whereby student ID cards would be accepted at the Larimer and Westminster campus libraries as library cards. Barcode placement and design, numbering sequences and the wording and placement of a statement on the back of the card to cover legal responsibility for library use had to be negotiated and coordinated between the college implementation committee, the card and equipment vendor, the campus student center, the public library and the city attorney.

A well-written agreement governing the joint-use library will define in broad strokes how the partners are to maintain a balance between operating independently and cooperating, but no agreement can anticipate how changes in personnel, technology, users, funding and philosophies will impact the joint-use library.

One of the key elements in maintaining a comfortable and productive balance in a joint-use library is having a defined process and schedule for evaluating the partnership. This process must encourage and reward openness and honesty.

Some questions to address in this process include–

- How do we define success?
- Is each partner meeting its financial obligations?
- Are the financial arrangements still fair?
- Is each partner operating to fulfill the vision of the joint-use library?
- Does either partner feel overwhelmed by the other?
- Do both partners recognize the value of the joint-use library?
- Are the needs of the different patron groups being met?
- Have changes in circumstances and needs been accommodated appropriately?
- How can we do this even better?

These discussions are also an opportunity to appreciate what each partner is contributing.

Additionally, the agreement should define a process for resolving conflicts. Disagreements in such a complex undertaking have to be expected and should not be interpreted as a sign of failure. From disagreement can come solutions that are as creative as the original intent and formation of the joint-use library.

CONCLUSION

Joint-use libraries develop out of a sincere commitment to provide the partner libraries' patrons with better service, a more functional facility, and improved resources. The libraries wish to use financial resources prudently. The partners are often inspired by a vision of a diverse community of users coming together at the joint-use library.

The partners quickly learn that they will have to give up control in some areas that seemed sacred and untouchable to reap the benefits of cooperating with another library. They will face unprecedented demands on their negotiation skills, time and patience. Some days, it may not seem worth the effort.

At the same time, librarians in joint-use libraries are given the opportunity to create something new and unique. They have the opportunity to interact with a new group of patrons and library staff. They learn new skills, master new areas of knowledge and learn to operate and thrive in a new organizational culture.

REFERENCES

City of Fort Collins and Front Range Community College. 1996. Intergovernmental agreement. Unpublished.

College Center for Library Automation. 1996. Establishing joint-use libraries. Report of the Standing Committee on Joint-Use Libraries (www.ccla.lib.fl.us/docs/reports/joint-use.pdf).

Conaway, Peggy. 2000. "One reference service for everyone?" *Library Journal* 125(12):42-44.

Dornseif, Karen, and Ellen Willis. 1999. "Making the joint-use library work: Harmony Library, Fort Collins, Colorado." *Colorado Libraries* 25(2):15-17.

Schwanz, Kathleen. 2000. "Thinking about a joint use library: a memorandum of agreement and a timetable can ensure success." *College and Research Libraries News* 61(6):478-480.

Reaching for a Vision: The Creation of a New Library Collaborative

Christina Peterson
Patricia Senn Breivik

SUMMARY. A new library, radically different in concept and reality from any library that currently exists, is being developed by the City of San Jose and San Jose State University. Located in downtown San Jose

Christina Peterson is Health Professions and Distance Learning Librarian, San Jose State University. She co-chairs the User Services Team which is engaged in planning all public services in the *new* Dr. Martin Luther King, Jr. Library, and is most intimately involved in planning reference, Web, distance, disabilities, and access to computer services. She has an MSLIS from Catholic University and a BS in Natural Resources from California State University, Humboldt.

Patricia Senn Breivik is Dean of the University Library at San Jose State University where collaboration efforts with San Jose Public Library are underway to open a merged library in 2003 that will serve as the Silicon Valley's 21st century information hub. Her academic degrees include DLS Columbia University, School of Library Service, New York, MLS Pratt Institute, Graduate School of Library & Information Service, Brooklyn, New York, and BA Brooklyn College, Brooklyn, New York. She serves as Chair of the National Forum on Information Literacy and is past President of the Fellowship of Christian Librarians and Information Specialists and the Association of College and Research Libraries. She also currently serves on the California State University Council Of Library Directors.

Address correspondence to: Christina Peterson, SJSU Library, One Washington Square, San Jose, CA 95192-0028 (E-mail: peterson@email.sjsu.edu) or Patricia Senn Breivik, SJSU Library, One Washington Square, San Jose, CA 95192-0028 (E-mail: pbreivik@email.sjsu.edu).

[Haworth co-indexing entry note]: "Reaching for a Vision: The Creation of a New Library Collaborative." Peterson, Christina, and Patricia Senn Breivik. Co-published simultaneously in *Resource Sharing & Information Networks* (The Haworth Information Press, an imprint of The Haworth Press, Inc.) Vol. 15, No. 1/2, 2001, pp. 117-129; and: *Joint-Use Libraries* (ed: William Miller, and Rita M. Pellen) The Haworth Information Press, an imprint of The Haworth Press, Inc., 2001, pp. 117-129. Single or multiple copies of this article are available for a fee from The Haworth Document Delivery Service [1-800-HAWORTH, 9:00 a.m. - 5:00 p.m. (EST). E-mail address: getinfo@haworthpress.com].

10.1300/J121v15n01_09

on a site of two earlier libraries, the new building will serve both the campus and the community. This paper provides the perspective of the Dean of SJSU Library, and a Reference Librarian heavily involved in the planning process. Issues addressed include initial and ongoing visions, barriers encountered, what works well in planning, merging vs. nonmerging of services, unexpected consequences, and hurdles left to clear. *[Article copies available for a fee from The Haworth Document Delivery Service: 1-800-HAWORTH. E-mail address: <getinfo@haworthpress.com> Website: <http://www.HaworthPress.com> © 2001 by The Haworth Press, Inc. All rights reserved.]*

KEYWORDS. Academic libraries, joint libraries, merged services, participatory planning, partnerships, project management, public libraries

INTRODUCTION

In 1996, San Jose State University President Robert L. Caret and San Jose Mayor Susan Hammer both faced similar problems: crowded main libraries badly in need of technological upgrades, with no space for expanding collections. Given the skyrocketing costs of building and maintaining libraries, neither leader had the financial resources to address these needs alone.

After comparing notes, the university president and the mayor reasoned: Why not join forces and build a new facility that could greatly improve library service to both the city and the university?

Following the public announcement in February 1997, dozens of people from the city and university, on advisory committees and task forces, began to think and talk seriously about the joint library. They considered where it would be located, what it would look like, what it should include, and how it would be operated. They also asked: What degree of jointness should there be? What aspects of the joint library should remain "separate"?

Spurred by the desire to see the project work, and understanding the value of hearing and considering opposing views, the city and university held town meetings, open forums and public hearings. They heard a wide range of opinions and ideas, from "Don't do it at all!" to "Build the structure jointly, but keep the libraries separate," to "Merge everything that it makes sense to merge."

In May of 1998 a memorandum of understanding was signed. The following November, California voters passed the education bond measure which included funding for the project, and the CSU Board of Trustees endorsed it. In December, an operating agreement was approved by the Academic Senate, President Caret, and the San Jose City Council. Both documents are available at www.library.sjsu.edu/jointlibrary.[1]

Now four years later and with approximately a year to go until opening, the 475,000 square foot Carrier Johnson designed building has already changed the downtown skyline of San Jose, and–amazingly for such a large and complex project (the total project cost is $177.5 million)–the construction remains on schedule and on budget.

Even more challenging is the operational and service planning that is moving ahead at a remarkable speed and which is also on schedule. There is still much planning to be finalized, but a lot more is now known about how things will work and what the benefits to the campus and community will be.

The perspective adopted for this article is twofold. The first is from Christina Peterson (CP), who has been a reference/liaison librarian at SJSU since June of 1986, and the second is from Patricia Senn Breivik (PSB), who came to SJSU in August of 1999 to serve as Dean of the University Library. A question and answer format is used to highlight issues of particular interest to librarians.

* * *

What was your initial reaction to the idea of a merged library?

(CP) Initially, the idea was intriguing: what would we have to accomplish to achieve a successful merger and how would we get there? As a born early adaptor and novelty seeker, I was attracted to the idea of developing a project that was totally new in the library world. After six months of introductory work with colleagues from both libraries, my reaction was mixed including a comprehension of the upheaval that would have to occur to achieve this bit of library history.

During this time the first User Services group came together to write shared goals for the new library and to review floor plans for optimum public services. We defined our user groups, services, and service points. We brainstormed new services that would grow out of the synergy of our merging. We endorsed seamless service although we were not sure exactly how close to that goal we would be able to come. We generated recommendations such as "Service staff should have strong input into the configuration of individual services points." Although, clearly, the original decision to merge was top-down, the team felt a strong desire to build a wide base of participation in the planning process. As a team, we were seeing a nascent trust and willingness to work together.

My personal reaction throughout this time was that, although I had to work hard to articulate what I had been doing as a user services librarian for many years and why I had done it in the manner that I did, this was valuable professionally.

(PSB) I had not planned to make another career change until I was contacted by the search committee which was seeking someone to guide this effort for SJSU. I was happily ensconced at a major research institution, but I was immediately intrigued about the possibility of a truly integrated academic/public library and its potential to be a national model for other metropolitan areas. After all, the American Association for Higher Education and other higher educational leadership have been promoting the importance of campuses becoming more engaged in their communities.[2] What a model this would be!

Moreover, as one who strongly believes in the role that librarians can play in moving "have-nots" into becoming "haves," I have increasingly become concerned about how traditional funding patterns for academic and public libraries are causing them to steadily lose ground in serving people. The reasons are obvious. The information explosion continues as does the unusually high inflationary rate on scholarly material. Libraries must have both the old and the newest technology. In addition to those financial challenges, every year there are more people to serve and a greater diversity of needs to be met. This new model might, I thought, offer at least a partial answer to the challenge of shrinking resources.

What is your vision for the library now?

(CP) The process has moved on considerably, including the formation of six hard-working planning teams: User Services, Collection Management and Technical Services, Organizational Design and Development, Online Systems and Technology, Administrative Services, and Policy and Procedures. These groups of librarians and staff from both libraries are creating the policies and guidelines that will turn the vision into a form of reality. My present vision incorporates the initial ideas of merged services with semi-merged and non-merged services to support new communities of readers and learners of all ages. We will be able to offer whole-person collections and services. The User Services Team now envisions innovative assistance such as in-building virtual reference, paging for academic patrons as well as public library customers, and a system of referral that will ensure the application of expertise to reference questions where needed. Other synergies are planned including outreach, information competence, and user training.

My vision has expanded to include how the two present library staffs will work together to provide user services. Our experience in the planning teams and sub-teams (twenty-one subteams under User Services alone!) shows that we can work together. We have weathered opposing viewpoints and philosophical differences but never shown reluctance to take part in the discussion! The teams have turned the participatory vision of the original planning groups into reality. Now we are working to bring all our colleagues into this wide participation model. The degree to which this can be accomplished will foretell the ease of day-to-day operation, assessment, and continued planning after opening day of the *new* King Library.

(PSB) Jane Light, SJPL Director, was the one who came up with the best analogy, i.e., our libraries are not being merged; rather they are being married. In a merger someone loses. In a good marriage, both partners retain their own personalities while at the same time supporting and enriching each other's lives. This vision also well incorporates the commitment that the whole will equal more than the sum of the two parts. We do not want to settle for whatever service is the better of the two existing practices. We want to forge a partnership that will allow us to offer more and better than what either of us is currently doing.

The co-managing or marriage partnering extends throughout the organization. Employees' institutional and union affiliations as well as their benefits will remain the same after merger as they are now; however, most operational units will be integrated and at least initially be co-managed with each co-unit head having designed lead responsibilities for specified functions within the unit. This means that all employees will have a primary supervisor who is from their parent organization, and most will also have a supervisor who will be from the other institution. The proposed organizational arrangement for the reference department, for example, appears in Illustration 1.

It is our hope that this kind of co-leadership will allow for a dynamic and professionally rewarding environment as well as a richer service base.

What practical benefits/pay-offs will it offer?

(CP) Obvious benefits include a larger staff with expanded expertise, a more comprehensive collection of books, journals, newspapers, lan-

ILLUSTRATION 1

Reference Services

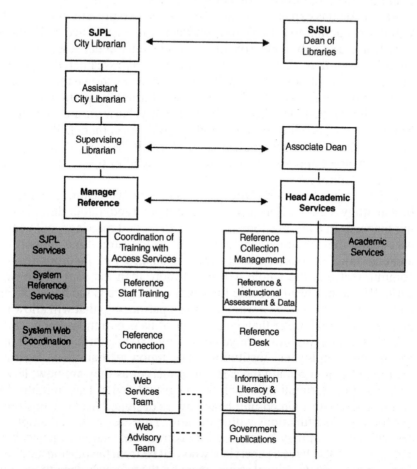

- **Web Advisory Team** will advise Web Services and the Web Service Manager. The team will be comprised of representatives from Information Technology, Access Services, Reference, Youth and Branch Services, and Marketing/Outreach.

Gray areas are not merged

guage materials, government publications, etc., a new infrastructure with state-of-the-art facilities, a new integrated online system, a library Website with entirely new information architecture based on usability studies, and a well thought-out service philosophy and vision. Benefits for the campus include additional materials such as a children's collection essential for the fields of education and library science.

(PSB) There are a few that immediately come to mind. From the community perspective, people will have ease of access to much richer holdings including onsite access to over 12,000 full text journals. In addition, I am excited about how the synergism of the public library's role as the poor person's university and the commitment of SJSU to first generation college students will eventually play out into a richer, more productive workforce for Silicon Valley–not to mention better quality of life for many families.

From the SJSU perspective, we will gain on-campus access to some additional resources (e.g., 33 foreign language newspapers in 19 different languages and 68 magazines in 17 languages) and the soon-to-be eighteen branch libraries which will allow our faculty and students, who live throughout the city, to have access to our resources and services without needing to drive to campus and to find a parking place. Hard copy materials requested will be delivered to them at their local library branch usually within 24 hours.

What were the greatest challenges in moving ahead?

(CP) Development of trust was a challenge, facilitated by enough staff with good will and desire to work together, objectivity provided by consultants at crucial stages, and top management's encouragement of the participatory process. Teams were charged with working out, owning, and presenting their recommendations for the best possible configuration of services in the *new* King Library and most achieved the requisite degree of trust in the course of that process. In any organization, whether dealing with extreme change or not, there are personality clashes, foot dragging, and downright sabotage. Between two organizations pushed into an initially reluctant marriage, these might have achieved the power to halt progress. Gossip in the halls can be particularly destructive since we still occupy separate halls (in two buildings a mile apart!). It is essential that we develop informal communication channels between us and the public library to keep the planning process running as smoothly as possible.

(PSB) Because this truly is a new undertaking, there are no models that can be adapted nor can it be proven in advance our marriage model will work. While this challenge has in recent years attracted unusually high quality librarian recruits, for many already on board it has been a time of deep concern–chief of which has been questions about how their abilities and long years of experience will fit into the as-yet-to-be-defined service structure.

What in the planning process was particularly difficult and how were those issues addressed?

(CP) The large combined staff of the new library and the comprehensive nature of the planning process presented difficulties. We all, at levels from top to bottom, were learning together how to handle a project of this size and magnitude. We needed project planning and management expertise! The chairs of planning teams were given training in project management and now think in term of timeline and deliverables. Uniform reporting document types were developed as was the policy approval process. Even though the scope of activities was new, we had an infrastructure of timeframe, reporting lines, phases, and project management that made sense.

Planning workload and anticipated work environment in the new building were difficult elements of the planning process. Even before the new library was a gleam in our eyes, we had some workload disparities. The planning teams needed to be led by people with a commitment to the project, leadership and consensus-building skills, facility at decision-making in a fast-paced environment, and good communication skills. Such people were already working at capacity in the pre-joint library environment before being recruited for planning teams. Individual workload adjustment, which had not been attempted in the past, was a necessity. Without it, the process would have foundered.

In addition, priorities for SJSU Library operation during planning were set. We needed guidance in which ongoing academic library services and functions would take precedence in the workload of the library as a whole and for individual librarians and staff. Also, the setting of academic responsibilities in the new library required that SJSU staff and librarians sit down together and create a statement that affirms the scholarly qualities and services that we value and want to bring into the *new* King Library, including information competence orientation, library liaison role to academic departments, continued employment of student assistants, and curricular orientation. These three processes:

workload modification, interim library priority setting, and academic responsibility statement, were essential in assisting individuals to assess and modify their work priorities and feel comfortable that the new work environment will include essential academic qualities.

(PSB) The sheer magnitude and complexity of the planning endeavor is daunting. The planning takes place under the direction of the Core Team, which is comprised of the Dean, Associate Dean and Project Manager of SJSU and the Director, Main Branch Supervisor and Project Manager of SJPL. We have also used the services of a number of consultants–both for joint planning efforts and to address needs just within our own library. Six jointly staffed and charged major planning teams, which eventually evolved into numerous task forces, have had to follow prescribed project-planning procedures, meet specific deadlines and keep coordinated. Every existing policy and procedure has to be compared and shaped into a recommendation for review by the Core Team.

To make the above possible a whole series of training events have been taking place including Myers-Briggs, project planning management, and policy and procedures writing. We also took time to explore the process of grieving related to change, to celebrate our library's past and to anticipate our future.

What has worked well in the planning process?

(CP) The planning process has brought out the best in both libraries, and many factors contribute to success. Most importantly, a large group of librarians and staff are committed to the success of the project. The sense that we were all learning together heightened the feeling of camaraderie amongst the rank and file. The Core Team showed tolerance for our learning curve, and we showed the same for theirs. Adequate time has been allotted to achieve appropriate levels of trust in the process and in colleagues in order to produce comprehensive policy recommendations and service guidelines. Formal and informal channels of communication have been worked out and will continue to serve well as the implementation and assessment phases commence. Project management training was offered and used which allowed this complex endeavor to be phased into parts: information gathering, analysis, recommendations, implementation. Dedicated project management professionals support the program and consultants were hired when neutrality or expertise were needed, e.g., the information architecture of the wholly *new* King Library Website and the organizational structure of the new library. An atmosphere of tolerance for new ideas and brainstorming prevails. Lastly, and not least, we laugh together, within teams, with the Core Team, and amongst ourselves, about the extra work and the unknowable aspects of the final result.

(PSB) Frequent and open communications in all directions have worked well in keeping people informed and efforts on track. The Core Team meets every other week as well as with the planning team co-chairs monthly and with all staff every other month. In addition, there is a monthly newsletter produced by staff, frequent e-mails are sent, and all Core and planning team meeting summaries are posted to our Intranet.

Have there been any unexpected consequences or benefits?

(CP) Of course there are many: speaking personally, there are the energizing nature of working together within a new conceptual framework, having a wide range of new colleagues, developing new skills in leadership, consensus building, priority setting and decision making. These are good. They are also consumptive of huge quantities of energy, so other consequences include overload, exhaustion, enforced tolerance of ambiguity, fears and anxieties about the new work environment. The place of *new* King Library planning activities within the retention, tenure and promotion process remains unclear to those of us working on tenure or promotion. One of the most empowering consequences is the realization that "we can do it!" We have taken on a huge job, and we are on schedule. This gives us the necessary organizational and personal confidence to face any difficulties that may arise after opening day.

(PSB) One of the things that has pleased me most is the quality of the University Library Board (ULB) of the Academic Senate. At every other university to which I have gone it has taken several years to attract senior level faculty to the library committee. Because of the campus concern for the new library, the newly charged ULB has the Academic Senate vice president/president elect as a member as well as strong faculty from the schools and colleges. ULB has been an essential partner as we have worked through difficult and politically challenging agendas.

What remaining hurdles do you anticipate?

(CP) Two sets of hurdles remain. We have less than one year to be ready to open our doors. We must keep on the same fast-paced schedule and maintain control of planning teams' and subteams' output. At the same time, the second set of hurdles arises through immersion in the very detailed nature of our planning process: it is now too easy to focus on interim goals and reports and forget the ultimate prize–our new library. In this environment, it is important to maintain our commitment and enthusiasm.

(PSB) We are racing the clock to be ready on time for the move in Summer 2003, and at the same time we continue to enhance our current campus services. This is also a difficult time financially in the State, and we have to hope that State and/or City budget cuts will not create hurdles beyond those that are already stretching our human and financial resources. Moreover, the move itself will require a level of orchestration worthy of a world class symphony. We shall be moving materials and staff into the new building from four locations and with much interfiling of materials. We also need to provide library and computer lab services during the moving in period when for approximately two months both our present and our future libraries will be closed. It should be exciting!

How will you evaluate the success of the merger?

(CP) Our good planning work will be measured by examining the appropriateness and extent of service outcomes to students, faculty, and community. Are students learning what they need to know of information literacy in order to achieve success in college and beyond? Is the library Website usable, informative, motivating? Are parents finding desired materials for their children and themselves? Is library programming useful to the community? Do librarians work productively with classroom faculty to develop curriculum that makes best use of library resources? We have benchmarked reference services separately in both libraries and will replicate these tests in the new library. Both libraries' Websites have been formally tested for usability; another round of testing will be conducted on the prototype Website for the new library. During the Fall semester, the incorporation of information literacy activities will be benchmarked in MUSE, the new freshman experience program, and will be examined again one year later. These tests will measure our service outcomes in the first year of the merged environment. Another important measure of success is how well we continue to work together to evaluate services, plan solutions to problems, and celebrate our triumphs. Will that co-chair of mine still be laughing with me over our difficulties and achievements a year after opening day? I predict that she will.

(PSB) There is an upfront commitment in the Operating Agreement to ensure that services in the new library are at least as good as currently exist. In addition, faculty were particularly concerned that opening academic resources to public users might cause higher loss rates and/or having materials checked out when needed by students for assignments. The public librarians, in turn, worry about our students checking out and keeping out all the computer manuals which are high use items in their library.

To address these concerns, the libraries working with a consultant have done bench marking in key areas against which we shall compare services in the new library. In addition to addressing concerns about availability of materials, the university collection is undergoing a complete inventory to ensure a clean database at move in and against which to measure collection loss. We shall also be working with our online system vendor to ensure statistical reporting that will allow ongoing monitoring of collection use by academic and community users.

Are there any lessons to be learned from this effort that are applicable to other library situations?

(CP) One of the most important lessons is the efficacy of the participatory model for planning. Although it requires more time to develop plans than does the top-down model, it achieves buy-in and ownership of service planning and implementation. In our situation, with two groups of unknown colleagues coming together to work on an enforced merger, broad participation since then and throughout the stages was essential in forming a staff who can develop a joint vision, plan for merged services, and share an understanding of different patron groups.

(PSB) My hope is that this project–in addition to enhancing library services for the campus and the community–will encourage other libraries to seek creative partnerships with other libraries and information providers in their areas so that limited resources can be stretched to better meet the information needs of those in need of our services and resources. We are doing our best to document our efforts and our accomplishments so that others can borrow from us whatever can work for them.

Any final thoughts?

(CP) It is ironic that the new library's operations and services are being planned within a strong participatory intent, when the original decision to develop such a library seemed more like an act of God or unstoppable environmental force. For myself, the importance lies in how we are asked to or choose to respond to decisions outside our own control. Without the initial top-down decision, we would have no ground-breaking library, extended collection, or new colleagues. Without the framework of participation in decision making, we would not have as good a service and operations model or as enfranchised a group of planners.

(PSB) The collaboration between our libraries is seen as a catalyst for additional collaborations with other libraries and agencies. In keeping with higher education concerns for campuses becoming more engaged in their communities, we believe the merging of the two libraries can afford a number of new opportunities to tie into community priorities. For example, we are working with campus personnel, local K-12 educators and community members to design a K-12 education resource center. It will bring town and gown together around issues related to enhancing K-12 education in San Jose.

* * *

As we review the above, we are struck by how many things have been left unsaid. We encourage readers to seek further information on the new King Library's Website at www.newkinglibrary.org, and to come visit us after we open! As SJSU President Caret stated, "This is the direction for the future. Libraries will become the informational hubs of our communities and gateways for access to our universities. What better place to start this trend than the Silicon Valley?"

REFERENCES

1. Klingberg, Susan, and Sylvia Hutchinson, "A library like no other for a community like no other: The joint library project of San Jose State University and the City of San Jose," San Jose State University marketing goldenrod brochure: 2.

2. Breivik, Patricia Senn, "Information Literacy and the Engaged Campus," *AAHE Bulletin*, 53 (November 2000): 3.

Staffing Challenges for a Joint-Use Library: The Nova Southeastern University and Broward County Experience

Harriett D. MacDougall
Nora J. Quinlan

SUMMARY. Nova Southeastern University and the Broward County Board of County Commissioners engaged in a cooperative agreement to build a joint-use library to serve the citizens of Broward County and the students, faculty, and staff of Nova Southeastern University. Two institutions

Harriett D. MacDougall is Director of the Library, Research, and Information Technology Center, Nova Southeastern University. She was the Director of the Einstein Library, the former main library at NSU. She holds a bachelor's degree in biology from Cedar Crest College, Allentown, PA, and a master's degree in library science from the University of South Florida, Tampa, FL. She is a member of ALA, ACRL and LAMA.

Nora J. Quinlan is Head of Reference and Access Services, Nova Southeastern University's Library, Research, and Information Technology Center. She holds a BA in History from Queens College, CUNY, an MS in Library Service and an MA in Art History from Columbia University. She is a member of the Rare Books and Manuscripts Section of ALA, and has served as program chair of the RBMS annual preconference in 1997 and 2002.

Address correspondence to: Harriett D. MacDougall, or Nora J. Quinlan, Library, Research, and Information Technology Center, Nova Southeastern University, 3100 Ray Ferraro, Jr. Boulevard, Ft. Lauderdale, FL 33314 (E-mail: harriett@nsu.nova.edu or nora@nsu.nova.edu, respectively).

[Haworth co-indexing entry note]: "Staffing Challenges for a Joint-Use Library: The Nova Southeastern University and Broward County Experience." MacDougall, Harriett D., and Nora J. Quinlan. Co-published simultaneously in *Resource Sharing & Information Networks* (The Haworth Information Press, an imprint of The Haworth Press, Inc.) Vol. 15, No. 1/2, 2001, pp. 131-150; and: *Joint-Use Libraries* (ed: William Miller, and Rita M. Pellen) The Haworth Information Press, an imprint of The Haworth Press, Inc., 2001, pp. 131-150. Single or multiple copies of this article are available for a fee from The Haworth Document Delivery Service [1-800-HAWORTH, 9:00 a.m. - 5:00 p.m. (EST). E-mail address: getinfo@haworthpress.com].

show that together they can provide more, and better, services to their constituents than they can separately. The authors have discussed one of the earlier challenges to making this joint-use library successful–creating a staff plan, recruiting, hiring, and training staff. The authors describe recruitment and hiring library staff for a joint-use library. *[Article copies available for a fee from The Haworth Document Delivery Service: 1-800-HAWORTH. E-mail address: <getinfo@haworthpress.com> Website: <http://www.HaworthPress.com> © 2001 by The Haworth Press, Inc. All rights reserved.]*

KEYWORDS. Broward County, Nova Southeastern University, joint-use library, staffing, recruiting, recruitment, hiring, cooperation, collaboration

In 2001 Nova Southeastern University's main library, the Einstein Library, faced the daunting challenge of more than doubling its staff and creating new departments in order to meet the needs of the University's soon to be opened new joint-use library. The library had to look for both creative and simple solutions to meet and implement these challenges. After developing a new staff plan, library staff established a set of criteria for the new positions and put into place a quick and efficient process of recruitment, interviewing, and selection of suitable candidates. With previous recruitment experience and an open-minded approach, the library's search committees hired more than fifty new staff members. In less than a year the library was successful in finding well-suited employees for its new facility.

BACKGROUND

Nova Southeastern University (NSU) is located in Fort Lauderdale, in Broward County, Florida. It is the largest independent institution of higher education in the southeast United States. As of 2001, it had over 19,000 students, with 15,048 in graduate or professional programs, and 4,019 as undergraduate students.[1] Started in 1964 with 17 graduate students, NSU quickly became aware of the needs of the non-traditional students it served.[2] These students requested advanced degree academic programs closer to home so they would not have to give up jobs or leave family members to pursue their academic degree. As working adults, they also wanted to apply their academic knowledge to the work situation. NSU was responsive to these students and by 1974 had become involved in distance education focusing on applied research. It quickly became a pioneer and leader in the distance education arena.

Today, 82% of the students at Nova Southeastern University attend classes in Florida; 72% of these are in Broward, Dade, or Palm Beach counties.[3] In addition, 4% of its students attend classes at NSU international sites, which include France, Greece, Venezuela, Canada, Panama, the Dominican Republic, Jamaica and the Bahamas. The Fischler Graduate School of Education and Human Services, The Graduate School of Computer and Information Sciences, the Wayne Huizenga Graduate School of Business and Entrepreneurship, and the Farquhar Center for Undergraduate Studies maintain extensive distance education programs. The university also maintains traditional campus-based programs with the Shepard Broad Law School, the Health Professions Division (which includes the Colleges of Osteopathic Medicine, Pharmacy, Dental Medicine, Optometry, and Allied Health), the Oceanographic Center, the Farquhar Center for Undergraduate Studies, and the Maxwell Maltz School of Psychology. It should be noted, however, that some portion of almost every school or center at NSU has a local, online or distance education component.

Community involvement at Nova Southeastern University has also been a theme at most of the schools or centers. Located on the main campus are the University School, a K-12 school, the Ralph J. Baudhin School for hearing impaired and autistic children, psychology clinics (also at the East Campus site), medical clinics in Broward and Dade counties, the Family Center, and the Institute for Learning in Retirement. NSU also offers community based instruction through its Communiversity program. In short, Nova Southeastern University offers "cradle to grave" educational opportunities for all ages and needs using a wide variety of delivery methods.

Broward County in southeast Florida is one of the fastest growing counties in the United States. A suburban/urban environment, it is home to over 1,668,000 people, making it the 14th largest county in the United States.[4] The population is ethnically diverse with 70.6% white, 20.5% black and 16.7% Hispanic. Long popular with retirees, 16% of the population is over 65. Recently there has been an influx of young families and 23.6% of the population is under 18. There are 249,923 students currently enrolled in the Broward County School District schools. In fact, Broward County is the largest fully accredited school district in the United States.[5]

The Broward County Libraries Division, a service of the Broward County Board of County Commissioners, is composed of thirty-six libraries. It includes the Main Library in downtown Fort Lauderdale, five regional libraries, twenty-seven branch libraries, and three reading rooms. A successful $139,900,000 bond issue in 1999 will add eleven more libraries by 2004. The library collection is over 2,500,000 items. The county library system has 950 employees and an annual budget of $46,000,000.[6]

A NEW JOINT LIBRARY

Nova Southeastern University's new main library is the Library, Research, and Information Technology Center, a joint-use facility with the Broward County Board of County Commissioners. It is the first of its kind–a cooperative agreement between a private university and a large county government. This agreement allows the residents of Broward County access to a wealth of library resources previously limited only to the students, faculty, and staff of Nova Southeastern University.

In 1997 Donald E. Riggs, the Vice President for Information Services and University Librarian at Nova Southeastern University, and Samuel F. Morrison, the Director of the Broward County Library, conceived the idea of a joint-use library. NSU was in the process of planning a new main library. Broward County Library has a long tradition of cooperative agreements with other entities in the community. It has worked with Broward Community College, the Broward County School Board, Florida Atlantic University, ArtServe, and other local agencies to bring better services to the community. Broward County Library has shown a strong commitment to outreach to the community, and has been both creative and aggressive in making its services better known and available to Broward County residents. Nova Southeastern University also has a long history of serving its local and distance students and in cooperating in the community. NSU has emphasized using technology as a tool to provide access to its library resources. In many ways, the idea of a new joint-use library was a natural partnership for the community.

FORMAL AGREEMENT

The agreement between Broward County and Nova Southeastern University for the design, construction, and operation of a joint-use library and parking garage, known as the Joint-Use Agreement,[7] was formalized on December 14, 1999. This agreement is unique in many ways. Nova Southeastern University hired the architect, Smallwood, Reynolds, Stewart, Stewart of Atlanta, and the contractor, Miller and Solomon, and oversaw the planning and construction of the building. Nova Southeastern University administers the building's use. The staff is employed by the university with one exception, the Head of the Public Library Services department, which is a joint appointment. Broward County funded half of the construction costs and it funds a portion of the ongoing operating expenses of the library and provides a portion of the acquisitions budget for the purchase of library materials. It might be said that Broward County has outsourced to NSU the operation of a research library for its county residents.

Construction began on the $43,000,000 facility in the summer of 2000. The building opened in October 2001 and had its grand opening on December 8, 2001. At 325,000 square feet, it is the largest library building in Florida. It stands five stories with the fifth floor scheduled to be finished by 2010. Electronic compact shelving is used on three floors in order to accommodate the projected 1,400,000 volumes it will hold at build out. The library has fourteen electronic classrooms, with one devoted to children and young adults and another two set aside for library training. It will have twenty electronic classrooms when the building is finally completed. Within the building is a 500-seat performing arts theater, which can be used for cultural events, lectures, performances, and academic debates or presentations. To accommodate faculty, staff, students, and Broward County residents, a café has also been included in the building. A very important feature of the building is the public library department area, which provides services comparable to a branch library in the Broward County Libraries system. This area has an activity room for story time, crafts and other special activities, a teen activity room, a large reading area, and popular library materials, including multi-media materials.

At the Library, Research, and Information Technology Center all NSU students, faculty, and staff and Broward County residents share the use of the facility. Seamless service to both groups was planned from the inception of the library. As in the Einstein Library, the previous NSU main library, students, faculty, and staff have all the privileges they would expect in an academic library. In the Einstein Library, the public was allowed walk-in access to the collection and to a few selected databases. Now Broward County residents, with proof of county residency, can obtain a NSU public library card, which gives them the following privileges: checkout of books and other library materials; access to 116 online commercial databases in the library of which 106 databases are available from home or work; booking of group study and conference rooms; use of interlibrary loan; intralibrary loan between NSU and Broward County Library locations; use of computer labs for word processing and other software programs; Internet access from any computer in the library; wireless access to the Internet, either with laptops that can be checked out, or with personal laptops with an authorized wireless card; reference assistance in person, by phone, or online; personal or group training on electronic resources; programs for youth, teens, and adults. The overriding principle is that all of the library's services will be fair and equitable. One user group will not be favored over the other.

CHALLENGES

There have been several early challenges to the new joint-use library. One of these is to clearly tell the story of this unique agreement. Although precisely stated in the Joint-Use Agreement, there has been confusion about who runs the library. It is not surprising, as the Agreement is a complex, fifty-four page document that few have committed to memory. It has also been the practice in most of the agreements in which Broward County has been a partner that the county has administered the agreement and the other partner has had more of a "silent" role. The reverse is true in this agreement. Nova Southeastern University owns and operates the joint-use library. It hires the staff and makes all the administrative decisions. It is also not always clear to public users why they must get a NSU public library card, rather than use their Broward County Library card. Although users are told this is because there are two different library systems, Innovative Interfaces for NSU and CARL for BCL, the convenience of one card is their primary desire. Equally confusing to Broward County resident users is the fact that they can use some NSU databases from remote locations but not all. NSU has made concerted efforts over the past several years, working with database vendors, to get permission for remote access for all users in the library–both university affiliated and public users. Not all vendors have agreed to this and some have restrictions on point of service. With time and hard work on getting the story out about this joint-use library, most of these challenges will be met.

STAFFING CHALLENGE

The most significant early challenge in providing outstanding library services in the new joint-use library was its staffing. The number of new positions needed, recruitment, and new staff training all had to be determined and accomplished in just over six months. Both the new staff and the library's original staff would need to provide both traditional and new services to a diverse user group of on-campus and distant students, faculty, staff, and the public. Many factors came into play in overcoming this challenge. It became apparent that because the Joint Use Agreement specified that the Library, Research, and Information Technology Center would be open to the public for 100 hours per week, significant additional staff would be required to effectively administer the building. The Einstein Library was open 90.5 hours per week, but because of its limited size and location, it served only a small group of on-campus students, faculty, staff, and some public users. The primary users of the Einstein Library were distance students and this was reflected in how the library was staffed. The two biggest departments were Document Delivery and Distance Library Services. With an almost 2,000% increase in space in the new library and the many new added features–fourteen electronic classrooms, public library services area, study rooms, conference rooms, café–it was expected that in-person use of the library would more than double. It was also expected that the largest increases would be in public users, some wanting to use the popular library materials and multi-media materials, but most wanting to use the advanced technology, research collections, and expertise of librarians with extensive experience with technology and research databases.

A NEW STAFFING PLAN

The Vice President for Information Services and University Librarian and the Director of the Library, Research, and Information Technology Center consulted with Broward County Library staff about the staffing needs for such a library. Neither of these NSU administrators has a background in public library services. They felt that NSU could benefit from the extensive knowledge of Broward County Library staff members who had previous experience planning joint-use libraries. Broward County Library staff members from the North Regional Library (a joint-use facility with Broward Community College) as well as Broward County Library senior staff members were consulted. The

Vice President for Information Services and the Director of the Library at NSU drew up a staffing plan, which included a new organizational chart. This plan would more than double the existing library staff and create new library departments. The plan called for the major increases in staff in the area of circulation, and created a new department for public library services. It also revived the reference department as a department separate from distance library services, and created new positions in administration. There were no increases in staff for interlibrary loan, distance library services or technical services.

The emphasis on increased use of the library which would impact the circulation department was based on the idea that there would be greatly increased needs for services in circulating materials, shelving, placement of reserves and holds, general greeting, and monitoring building use. The circulation desk would be the focal point on the first floor for providing directions and most of these basic services. Circulation would be the only department staffed during all of the hours that the library was open.

The library administration believed that there would be an increased demand for reference service. The number of reference staff was increased dramatically to provide a high level of service for face-to-face, call-in, or online reference services. It was also expected that the reference librarians would take on the bulk of collection development to select quality materials to build the collection to 1,400,000 volumes. They would also be responsible for handling the increased amount of in-house library instruction and tours for students, faculty, and Broward County residents. Job descriptions for the positions in reference were written to be quite general. This would allow the "widest net" to be cast by the search committee to be able to recruit those best suited for these positions.

In administration, positions were added for facilities management and personnel management. Both of these positions were taken out of the staff plan, but the facilities manager was re-introduced after the building was opened. Demand for use of the library building has been so positive that the facilities manager was found to be an essential position.

PUBLIC LIBRARY SERVICES

Planning the public library services department was very critical to the success of library services in this joint-use library. Staff members from the Broward County Library were consulted about the space and about the staff plan. Their recommendations were used to create spaces for reading areas, book stacks, multi-media areas, a teen activity area, and an activity room for youth. A staffing plan was created that has the head of public library services in a joint appointment, reporting to both Broward County Library and NSU. This position was very important to the success of public library services. It was determined that the person in this position should have extensive work experience with Broward County Library. With this experience he or she would be able to facilitate communication with Broward County Library and be able to tailor NSU's public library service to that of Broward County Library to make services as seamless as possible for Broward County users. It was clear that the person who filled this position would need to recruit twelve staff members (eight librarians and four paraprofessionals) quickly and be able to create programs that would draw people into the new library. During a time of a severe shortage of youth services librarians, this appeared to be a formidable recruitment challenge.

HIRING KEY STAFF

The first two key staff members to be hired were the Head of Reference and Access Services and the Head of Public Library Services. The former would have as a first responsibility the recruitment of the largest number of staff (13 librarians and two paraprofessionals in reference as well as overseeing the hiring of staff for Circulation). Therefore it was determined that the position of Head of Reference and Access Services should be filled first. A search committee was formed, ads were sent out, and resumes were reviewed. Several candidates were chosen for interviews. A list of questions was drawn up that emphasized the ability to manage staff, the ability to organize large projects, knowledge of current practices and use of technology in libraries, the ability to manage successfully in a dynamic, changeable environment, and experience with recruitment and with academic search committees. From this group three candidates were invited for a full day campus interview.

The final candidate chosen had all the attributes the search committee identified as important for success in this position. It seemed to be helpful in this case that the person chosen for the position was an internal candidate. The successful candidate brought a strong knowledge of the "culture" of the organization, a strong understanding of the goals of the joint-use library, and knowledge of the planning that preceded the actual construction of the new library building.

For the position of Head of Public Library Services, it was determined that an employee from the Broward County Libraries system would be most successful in this position. Broward County Library staff members have extensive experience with partnering, programming for public patrons, and publicizing and promoting library services. The Vice President for Information Services at Nova Southeastern University asked the Broward County Library Director to identify librarians at the appropriate level of experience to be considered for this position. A search committee consisting of staff from both NSU and Broward County Library considered four librarians. Phone interviews followed by an on-site campus interview were conducted. After a thorough selection process, a Broward County librarian, with many years of management experience at Broward County Library, was selected for this position.

RECRUITMENT PROCESS

With these two critical positions filled by the spring of 2001, staff recruitment was started in earnest. From the beginning, it was determined that the new library would present seamless services to the patrons–Broward County residents and NSU students, faculty, and staff. Therefore, the search committee for the public library services department would include staff from Broward County Library and two NSU librarians. The latter were able to bring their knowledge of the NSU Library search committee process and information about the University to the search committee. This search committee also provided an early example of collaboration between the two libraries to meet the goals for excellent and seamless library services for all. It was determined early in the process that NSU would avoid competing with Broward County Library for new librarians whenever possible in the recruitment process. NSU was aware that Broward County Library had a large ongoing recruitment effort due to the rapid expansion of new libraries in the system. It was felt that this non-competitive attitude would encourage good working relationships with Broward County Library. Both libraries even recruited side-by-side at the ALA Job Placement Center, and resumes, information, and well wishes were shared. NSU recruiters did not turn away resumes from Broward County librarians, but potential candidates working at Broward County Library were never solicited.

In the late spring of 2001, search committees were formed to fill the new, professional positions planned for the library. The majority of these positions were in the reference department and the public library services department. Other than the two new department heads, there were eight new librarian positions in the public library services department and thirteen new librarian positions in the reference department–two for reference/instruction; three for reference/subject specialist; seven for general reference; one for Webmaster librarian. The original intent was to have five separate search committees. It quickly became apparent that this would be difficult to administer, as the search committee chair for four of the positions would be the same person. The other difficulty was, with a limited staff of librarians to serve on search committees, there would be a great deal of overlap in committee membership. It was determined that the three search committees for reference positions could be combined into one committee. One advantage of this was that since many applicants asked to be considered for all the reference positions (whether or not they qualified), they could be reviewed once rather than several times. All applicants for the three categories of reference librarians were put into one pool. Each applicant was reviewed for all of the available positions for which he or she had expressed interest. Additionally, with a candidate's permission, the candidates could be considered for any other positions in the library for which they were qualified.

REFERENCE SEARCH COMMITTEE

The original plan for the search committee for the reference positions included six librarians. The chair was the new Head of Reference and Access Services. Included on the committee were the Head of Document Delivery, the East Campus Branch Librarian, the North Miami Beach Branch Librarian, and two reference librarians from reference. One of the reference librarians, however, applied for one of the positions, creating a conflict of interest, and another librarian went on maternity leave. This left four librarians and the chair as a search committee. Although small, it was decided that the committee size would allow for greater flexibility. It would be easy to arrange meetings to schedule phone interviews, and to arrange dates for candidates to visit the campus. The search committee chair used e-mail and conference calls to stay in touch with the committee, sometimes in lieu of face-to-face meetings. One member of the search committee had a very active travel schedule, teaching distance students information literacy skills. Because the university has an 800 number, this search committee member was able to call in from anywhere in the United States to join the group as needed. All of these techniques allowed the search committee to "meet" quickly, make decisions, and further the search process.

RECRUITMENT

With a timeline of opening the new library by October 2001, leaving just six months to fill positions, it was decided early in the search process that positions would only be posted to listservs and Websites rather than advertised in the more traditional journals and professional publications. This decision was based on the cost of advertisements, the slow turnaround time in getting ads published, and an interest in candidates who were technologically adept enough to rely on the Internet to do a job search. The specific listservs were identified based on special needs of each position. Positions were also posted on the Florida Library Jobline. In previous searches, it was discovered that this jobline was very effective in finding candidates who are interested in making a professional move within, or to, Florida. Surprisingly when jobs were posted in this way, many other Internet sources, including sites for library schools, picked up the positions and posted them on their sites, which helped to spread the word about openings.

The library had also previously been very successful in recruiting candidates at the ALA Job Placement Center. Consistent with its previous experiences, the job placement center was used at ALA Midwinter and Annual meetings. The chair of the search committee also approached ACRL about conducting a placement center at their national meeting in 2001 in Denver. The head of the search committee found the placement centers an excellent way to "get the pulse of the market," get the word out, and learn what candidates needed to know about the joint-use library and the positions available. It also gave the search committee chair and the other active recruiters an opportunity to practice telling the story of the new joint-use library and the numerous new positions. It was discovered through this process that candidates wanted much more information about the south Florida area, particularly about Broward County, and they needed more information about Nova Southeastern University.

SEARCH PROCESS

The process of the search was similar in many ways to previous Einstein Library search committees, except in the quantity of applications received. Nearly 200 candidates were reviewed for the reference librarian positions alone. As resumes were received, they were copied, and distributed to the appropriate search committees and to the office of human resources at the university. An ongoing log of applicants was maintained which included an action item for each applicant. The log was updated if applicants withdrew or were not qualified for positions. Search committee members were given review sheets for each position to be used while considering application materials. The review sheets contain minimum and preferred requirements for each position laid out in a grid that made it easier for committee members to remember and review these requirements. The review sheets made it easier to eliminate, compare, and rank each candidate and it guaranteed that committee members had reviewed all of the applicants in a pool, lessening the possibility of a candidate being skipped or "lost."

INTERVIEW PROCESS

The reference search committee met approximately every other week to discuss applicants. Each candidate's eligibility and status for the positions was reviewed. Committee members debated applicants' strengths and weaknesses and applicants were compared and ranked. If there was no consensus on a candidate, the application was set aside for future review. The pool of successful applicants was then considered for a telephone interview. In the interest of time and money, and to ascertain the level of technical skill of the candidate, e-mail was used to distribute information before the telephone interview. The e-mail message to candidates invited for a phone interview specified the position for which the person was being considered, explained the telephone interview process, and gave available dates and times for the interview. Also included were links to the library's main Web page, a link to the Web page for the new library, links to promotional and informational publications from the university, and a link to the instructional manual developed as a training tool for students. In the past, some of this information had been mailed to candidates, which could delay the search process.

Telephone interviews were structured to last no more than thirty minutes. The search committee created a list of questions specific to each position. Search committee members met either in person or via conference call to conduct the phone interview. At the appointed time, the candidate was called and put on speakerphone. Questions were the same for every candidate. The order of questions was meant to gauge the applicant's knowledge of the position and the institution first, and to give them time to relax. Next the search committee was interested in the candidate's work style, initiative, and experience. The questions then became more focused on the position, technical skills, and dealing with the challenges of the job. One of the last, and often unexpected questions was "If you were offered this position, what would be your reasons for not accepting the position?" This often elicited interesting responses and let the candidate know that the search committee wanted to know their true level of interest in the position.

ON-CAMPUS INTERVIEWS

After the telephone interviews, campus interviews were set up with candidates who were considered suitable for the positions. For positions in reference and in public library services, a full day interview was scheduled. Candidates were invited to visit the campus in Ft. Lauderdale. As part of the daylong interview, candidates chosen for interview for reference positions were asked to prepare a presentation to demonstrate their skill in doing bibliographic instruction to a group of students. The candidates for youth services librarian were asked to prepare a presentation for children or young adults, including a storytelling and/or a craft project. Each candidate was asked to do a presentation lasting 15 to 20 minutes. This was then followed by a question and answer session with the audience. Library staff members were asked to serve as an audience for these presentations and to evaluate the candidate. Each candidate was given a chance to interact with as broad a segment of the library staff as possible. In addition, the candidate spent time with the search committee members.

With library staff members invited to all of the search committee presentations, library staff from reference, technical services or document delivery might be included in storytelling or craft presentations and library staff members from youth services might attend a presentation on a variety of databases or a topic of interest for library instruction. Broad participation by library staff in the search committee process assisted in creating a more open, collaborative environment, an understanding of what other library staff members were doing, and ultimately a more fully integrated staff. Although all library staff members attended the presentations and evaluated candidates, only the search committee completed the final, formal assessments and made recommendations to the library director.

Many factors were considered when selecting new staff members for the joint-use library. It was important to hire library staff that had some experience in working with both academic and public users. If it was not possible to find both types of library experience, the search committee looked for librarians with a desire to work with both user groups. Traditionally public librarians respond to reference inquiries with an "answer" and academic librarians teach users how to find the answer. In this new joint-use library the plan was to find a blend of the two approaches–to give the answer as needed and to encourage further learning with a high service attitude and an engaging environment in which to learn library skills. It was therefore important to select library staff with very good skills in reference and public services, technology, teaching, and customer service.

The process of reviewing resumes, telephone interviews and on-campus interviews continued though the summer of 2001 as the construction of the library building progressed. By late summer, the contractor gave Nova Southeastern University October 1, 2002 as the date the new library could be occupied (this date was later revised to October 8, 2001). It was decided that September 4, 2001 would be the starting date for as many of the new library staff as possible.

HIRING SUPPORT STAFF

While the searches for professional librarians progressed, the library staff member in charge of circulation was actively seeking the best-suited candidates as support staff. As stated earlier, in order to provide some basic services in the new joint-use library, one of the largest increases in staff was to be in the circulation department. There was some concern early in the process that these positions would be very difficult to fill and that retention would be a challenge. The reason for this concern was that the position of library assistant is one of the lowest paying jobs in the library. Surprisingly over 85% of these positions were filled by the summer of 2002, and the retention rate thus far has been almost 100%. The staff members selected for these positions have very good customer service skills and they have been successful in working with academic and public users.

ORIENTATION AND TRAINING

With so many people starting in new positions at one time it became imperative to develop a comprehensive training and orientation program. By the end of August 2001, nearly as many new professional staff had been hired as there were professionals currently employed in the Einstein Library. The mission, purpose and practices of the Einstein Library had to be transmitted to the new staff and they had to be quickly integrated into the pre-existing group so that their transition to the new building could be quickly and efficiently accomplished. A newly created staff training program was developed out of the necessity of training such a large number of staff members at the same time. The training program created had to be general enough to include all new library staff members, both professional and paraprofessional, for at least some portion of the training orientation.

With a start date for many new staff the first week of September, and the move-in date set for October 8, 2001, there were several weeks to train new staff members. Of serious concern was where to house the new staff until the move to the new library. Because of a severe space shortage, the Einstein Library had no extra space and there was no other office space readily available on campus. It was finally decided that "borrowing" a microcomputer lab from the information technology department at NSU was the best solution. This lab was located on the second floor of the Parker Building, just upstairs from the Einstein Library. The new staff would have access to computers for training and to the Internet and they would be in close proximity to the Einstein Library. This would allow them easy access to its services and staff. The only problem was that the lab was not available in the evenings or weekends as classes were scheduled to use it then. Therefore, no personal items, library materials, or supplies could be left in the lab at the end of the day.

The training program started with a general orientation and introduction to the university and the library. Training was divided into three parts. Department heads were asked to do a presentation on what their department did and how they operated. They were asked to introduce their staff and describe their department's services and do a demonstration or train (if needed) the new staff. For instance, the Head of Distance and Instructional Library Services did a presentation about how library services are provided to distance students. The Head of Reference and Access Services did a training session on the grants and foundations collection. The Assistant University Librarian for Systems demonstrated the online catalog, NovaCat, and issued staff mode accounts.

Not only library staff was involved in the training program. The NSU Office of Information Technology staff did presentations about the University's e-mail system. The Human Resources Office scheduled a special orientation program for all new library staff.

Because NSU library has offered so many of its resources online, a large portion of the training was to be done by database providers. Working with the Head of Collection Development, a wish list for vendor training was drawn up. Vendors such as ProQuest, Gale, Bowker, CSA, Ovid, FirstSearch, and Wilson were contacted and invited to send a trainer to campus. Almost all accepted the invitation to visit and they were willing to cover their costs. A few vendors insisted on being reimbursed for their travel expenses. The library felt that this was inappropriate and decided to do the training for these vendor products with library staff instead. One vendor who was having financial difficulty offered a Web based training session. This opportunity to use a training modality that would simulate one that might be done by the distance library services staff was eagerly embraced. It was seen as a good way to demonstrate how distance students might be trained.

The third portion of the training program was tours of the libraries affiliated with NSU, including The Health Professions Division Library, the Law School Library, the Oceanographic Library, and branch libraries at the East Campus and North Miami Beach. A half-day visit was also planned for a visit to the Broward County Main Library in downtown Ft. Lauderdale. Here new NSU staff met the administrative and department staff, and learned about the services and resources available through Broward County Library.

All of these activities were scheduled over a three-week period. In addition to the department presentations, vendor training, and tours it was decided to give the new staff members a special project to work on in spare time. All of the library's Web pages had to be restyled to meet the new University standard. This was a large undertaking that could not be done by one person or by current staff who were too busy with the incipient move to the new library. A template was developed and sections of the Web pages were divided up among the new staff.

On September 4, 2001, the new staff arrived to begin working. The Vice President and Library Director made welcoming remarks. Orientation packets were handed out and a welcome luncheon was served. In the afternoon library staff escorted the new staff to the Office of Human Resources where paperwork was processed, University IDs obtained, and e-mail accounts set up.

While the training program was underway, library staff continued the work of planning the move to the new library. The tragedy of September 11, 2001 affected everyone at NSU and repercussions were felt immediately for the training program. Vendors scheduled for training could not or would not travel. The training schedule was quickly rearranged to accommodate all of the changes. Some vendors offered alternative modes of training. One vendor whose staff was in Baltimore did training over a speakerphone. Others postponed to a later date and library staff stepped in to do overviews.

In the end, despite these setbacks, the training program was successful. New staff met and heard from all the key players at NSU and Broward County Library. They had the opportunity to work with the library staff, and tour all of the libraries affiliated with NSU and Broward County Main Library. They learned many of the major databases that the library offered. The new staff quickly became familiar with the library's Web pages by actually working on them. Finally, they were integrated into the transition to the new building by helping with the move. By October 8, 2001, opening day of the new library for students and faculty, the newly hired staff members became part of the new joint-use library and seamlessly filled their positions to welcome library users.

OBSERVATIONS/CONCLUSIONS

When asked to write about this cooperative project–a joint-use library–the authors were aware that it was very early in the process to be drawing any conclusions about the effectiveness of the overall project. However, there was a desire to write about the beginnings of the project and some of the early challenges, most specifically the staffing challenges. Since the two authors were very active in tackling the staffing challenges, it was decided that this could be described accurately. We felt that it was important to talk about how a cooperative project was addressed and the steps that were taken to accomplish the goal of staffing this library.

Although the library has been open for less than ten months, and an assessment of its effectiveness will not be available for some time, the operation in the early months has been very smooth. The staff selected for this new library has shown enthusiasm for working with both public and academic patrons. Library users, both academic and public, have let it be known that they are well pleased with "their" library. While many academic libraries are seeing a decline in basic statistics–library materials checked out, reference questions–the joint-use library statistics are showing marked increases in these areas. Over fifty percent of materials checked out have been by public patrons, and there is an increase in materials checked out to academic users compared with the statistics for the last reporting period. Other noticeable increases include an 82.5 percent increase in the number of reference questions asked and a 24.4 percent increase in the number of interlibrary loan transactions.

Along the way to meeting the goals set for the joint-use library, there were some adaptations and changes, and some of the goals have not yet been met. The staff plan for the public library services area required several adjustments. A position for an assistant head of public library services was created to provide more day-to-day management of this area. Another position of A-V Librarian was established when it was discovered that there was a great interest in these media. The position of library Web master changed over the course of a year, as the duties for this position expanded and became more technologically sophisticated. There are still several positions that remain unfilled. The nationwide shortage of librarians and a temporary job freeze after September 11, 2001 have had an effect on finding suitable staff to fill some positions. Not surprisingly the librarian positions remaining unfilled are for two youth services librarians, a reference librarian specializing in instruction, a reference librarian specializing in the sciences, and a Web master librarian.

Having been closely involved in this collaborative project from the talking stages, there are some observations that can be made. The care and detail with which the agreement was drawn has been an important part of the process. The agreement was carefully conceived and executed, with exact details pertaining to funding and possible scenarios. Without a carefully crafted agreement, misunderstandings could have caused a downfall before the collaboration started. It was important that the vision and goals for the joint-use library be embedded in all the plans and actions related to the joint-use library. In the case of this library, it was a goal to provide seamless service to both academic and public users. From the first building plans, through the staffing, this goal was kept in the forefront. Finally, it is important to "tell the story" of the agreement and the joint-use library as often, and in as many different settings as possible. Because it is the first of its kind, a private with public joint-use library agreement, the story must be repeated. It is evident that even library staff members from Broward County Library and from NSU libraries are confused about the breadth of the user group and other aspects of this cooperative agreement. In writing this article the authors have attempted to tell one part of the story of this new joint-use library.

REFERENCES

1. NSU Fact Book, http://www.nova.edu/cwis/urp/factbook/2001/.

2. Goldstein, Stephen L., The search for Nova University: an essay on its first twenty-five years 1964-1989. Fort Lauderdale, FL: Nova University, 1989.

3. NSU Fact Book.

4. U.S. Census Bureau. State and County QuickFacts. http://quickfacts.census.gov/qfd/states/12/12011.html.

5. Broward County Public Schools. District Overview. http://www.browardschools.com/about/Default.htm.

6. Broward County Libraries. Bond Issue Update. http://www.broward.org/library/bond.htm.

7. Agreement Between Broward County and Nova Southeastern University, Inc. For Design, Construction, And Operation Of A Joint-Use Library And Parking Garage. [n.p.] 1999.

Index

http://www.haworthpress.com/store/product.asp?sku=J121
© 2001 by The Haworth Press, Inc. All rights reserved.
10.1300/J121v15n01_11

For Product Safety Concerns and Information please contact our EU representative GPSR@taylorandfrancis.com Taylor & Francis Verlag GmbH, Kaufingerstraße 24, 80331 München, Germany

Batch number: 08153797

Printed by Printforce, the Netherlands